LATIN AMERICAN CINEMA

Film and History

UCLA LATIN AMERICAN STUDIES

Volume 26

Series Editor: Johannes Wilbert

Editorial Committee

Robert N. Burr
Thomas J. La Belle
Gerardo Luzuriaga
James W. Wilkie, Chairman

LATIN AMERICAN CINEMA
Film and History

E. Bradford Burns

UCLA LATIN AMERICAN CENTER
University of California • Los Angeles
1975

Copyright © 1975 by The Regents of the University of California
All rights reserved

Cover photograph is of a *cangaceiro* from Glauber Rocha's
film *Deus e o Diabo na Terra do Sol.*

Library of Congress Catalog Card Number: 74-025244
International Standard Book Number: 0-87903-026-7
Printed in the United States of America

Preface

Film is an invaluable teaching device; it also has great potential for historical research. For more than a decade, I have maintained an interest in it, first for my teaching and only later for my research. My first experiments with it to enhance my courses in Latin American history were sporadic and somewhat impulsive. Intuitively I appreciated the importance of the image, but it took many years before I developed a methodology for properly incorporating films into the curriculum.

Becoming bolder the past two years, I centered some of my Latin American history courses on films, rather than relying on an occasional movie to expand or clarify lectures and discussions. My first such experiment during the winter quarter of 1973, with a course entitled Latin American Social History, received a warm endorsement from 280 students who enrolled in it. Thus encouraged, I repeated the course the following year and added two seminars, one for freshmen on film and history and another for seniors on documentary film as a source for historical research. I am currently experimenting with another course, this one using Brazilian films as a means of studying Brazilian history.

As I groped my way through these experiments, I became acutely aware of the dearth of methodological and conceptual studies for the use of film as an historical tool and the lack of bibliographic and filmographic guides to orient those who may want to combine film and history. This book, varied as it is in structure, is a handbook offering some of the basic orientation needed by those embarking on similar experiments with the use of film. It is a brief introduction which I hope will serve as a springboard for further and more intensive studies.

Film is fascinating. My own experiments with its use in the classroom indicate that it generates lively and substantive discussions. It ignites students' imaginations. It presents a view of Latin America which my lectures cannot duplicate.

In the preparation of this book I am particularly indebted to the University of California Committee on Innovative Projects in

University Instruction which for two years funded my experiments with the use of film in the classroom. The UCLA Office of Academic Change and Curriculum Development has been equally generous and encouraging. Similar support came from my colleagues in the Department of History, UCLA, and when there was a pinch for funds the Department came through with the needed money. Professor Johannes Wilbert, Director of the Latin American Center, UCLA, supported these experiments with the use of film. The logistical, financial, and moral support of the Center has been a great source of encouragement.

My students — and the teaching assistants — have also been enthusiastic and helpful. They cheerfully submitted to the experiments and any successes resulted from their invaluable input. They taught me a great deal. It is my hope that the chapters that follow will help and encourage others who wish to incorporate film into the study of Latin America.

E. Bradford Burns

Hollywood Hills
October 1, 1974

Contents

Preface		v
1.	A Filmic Approach to Latin America's Past	1
2.	On the Theory of Film as History	
	Film and History: Some Thoughts on Their Interrelationship	47
	Eugene C. McCreary	
	Film and Style: The Fictional Documentary	67
	Joan Mellen	
3.	On Student Views of Film as History	93
	Film for the Historian	94
	Beth August	
	Historical Continuity through Film: The Example of Bolivia	100
	Bill Taylor	
	The Fictional Documentary: Two Analyses of *Blood of the Condor*	105
	1. Bil Wadum	105
	2. Magi Fainer	108
4.	In Search of Films	112
5.	Bibliographies	116
	Conceptualizing the Use of Film to Study History: A Biblio-Filmography	116
	Bibliography of Latin American Cinema	125

1

A Filmic Approach to Latin America's Past

1

History records human action through time; it is the memory of human group experience. Although that memory and its records have taken many forms, scholars have demonstrated a strong preference for the written word both in their search for the past and in their reconstruction of it. The written word acquired such sanctity that it is difficult to conceive of other means of studying the past. Unfortunately devotion to tradition has blinded Clio's disciples to the many technical innovations of the twentieth century which could be employed advantageously to explore, study, and recreate the past. Most notable of the neglected innovations is the film.

When the moving picture first astounded and delighted the public at the end of the nineteenth century, a few of its pioneers recognized it at once to be a major ally for historians. W. K. L. Dickson, who played a vital role in the development of the Edison motion picture cameras, thought the action and excitement of the film, with its unique advantage of visually preserving great events, would replace the "dry and misleading accounts, tinged with the exaggerations of the chroniclers' minds." Films, in his opinion, would enrich our archives and enliven our study of history.[1] Others supported his views. For example, the early Parisian movie house entrepreneur Boleslaw Matuszewski promoted the motion

---

[1] For information on the early contributions of Dickson see V. F. Perkins, *Film as Film: Understanding and Judging Movies* (Baltimore: Penguin, 1972), pp. 42, 43, 47.

picture as "a new source of history" and proposed the establishment of film archives for the use of historians.[2] During those early years, the pioneer filmmakers concentrated on capturing actuality: a train arriving in a station, pedestrians on a crowded street, national figures making public appearances, and family scenes. Between mid-July 1898, when Brazilians first began to make films, and mid-1908, they shot only "natural scenes." The initial phase of the Mexican film industry, 1896-1917, concentrated almost exclusively on capturing "reality" as the human eye perceived it. As though propelled by the Positivist philosophy so dominant in Mexico by the end of the nineteenth century, the early filmmakers tried to use the camera as one means of seeing and recording the truth. Even their early historical films purported to be "true history" according to the rigorous tenets of Positivism. Before very long, however, filmmakers discovered that the "magic" of the camera could be used to create illusion, fantasy, and the atypical characteristics that enticed an intrigued public into the movie houses. The camera became a magic wand creating illusion. Thereafter, it tended to avoid reality. Little wonder then that the scholar shied away from the film during the early decades of its development, a neglect that continued despite filmmakers' later renewed concern with reality.

By the 1920s, some filmmakers were turning back to the original purpose of the film: to capture and transmit reality. Two major figures appeared, Robert Flaherty and John Grierson, whose ideas and films firmly established a documentary tradition. In many ways they aligned themselves with concerns of the historians. Flaherty, credited as the originator of the factual film, was the careful observer, insistent his material be filmed on its actual location using real people, not actors. His first film, *Nanook of the North,* released in 1922, at once revealed the power of the camera to capture life-styles and human drama. In the following years, Flaherty made other films which consolidated his reputation for the poetic capture of the life-styles of ordinary people engaged in their daily dramas.

---

[2]Fritz Terveen, "Film as a Historical Document," *Film and the Historian,* a combined reprint of *University Vision,* No. 1, February, 1968, and the monograph *Film and History,* April, 1968 (London: British Universities Film Council, 1969), p. 22.

John Grierson applied theory to the emerging film form. Although many definitions of documentary were put forth, Grierson's idea that it is <u>the creative depiction and interpretation of reality</u> still seems as viable as it is simple and useful. With a determined social conscience, he boldly pointed to the path for future documentary filmmakers to follow. He summarized his principles as three:

> (1) We believe that the cinema's capacity for getting around, for observing and selecting from life itself, can be exploited in a new and vital art form. The studio films largely ignore this possibility of opening up the screen on the real world.... Documentary would photograph the living scene and the living story. (2) We believe that the original (or native) actor, and the original (or native) scene, are better guides to a screen interpretation of the modern world.... (3) We believe that the materials and the stories thus taken from the raw can be finer (more real in the philosophic sense) than the acted article.[3]

The documentary filmmaker, according to Grierson, enjoyed the right to interpret his materials. Indeed, it was incumbent upon him to do so. His very selection of the footage and his editing of it injected a subjective interpretation. As Grierson succinctly noted, "You photograph the natural life, but you also, by your juxtaposition of detail, create an interpretation of it."[4] He dialectically united impersonal observation (what the camera sees) with personal participation (how the filmmaker interprets what the camera sees). The documentary is the result of such dialectics.

What Grierson had to say was fundamental, but it was by no means the last word on documentaries. Future generations of filmmakers debated, refined, and expanded the practice and theory bequeathed by Flaherty and Grierson. Much of their concern focused on the concepts of reality. Both film theorists Erwin Panofsky and Andre Bazin noted that the basis of the medium of film is photographic and that the photograph is the image of reality or nature. In that sense the camera faithfully captures on film whatever it confronts. The camera discovers

---

[3]Forsyth Hardy (ed.), *Grierson on Documentary* (New York: Praeger, 1971), pp. 146-147.

[4]*Ibid.*, p. 149.

rather than creates. Some filmmakers exalt this quality of the camera to preserve accurately on film whatever it sees. To them, film shows life as it is. The film gives form to the human experience and dramatically communicates it. The filmmaker and theorist Dziga Vertov, an outstanding representative of a vigorous documentary movement in the Soviet Union, considered film as "a world perceived without a mask, as a world of naked truth (that cannot be hidden)."[5] Filmmakers recognize that it is possible to "fool" the camera with lighting, make-up, positioning, and so forth, but documentary filmmakers reject the temptation to do so, at least for the sake of conscious deception. They obviously select what they want the camera to record and which footage they want to retain. For those reasons, <u>few would support the idea that the film as edited and projected is objective; most agree it is subjective.</u> The filmmakers reveal an honesty in that respect which social scientists could emulate.

Although much of the documentary filmmakers' work, thought, and goals parallel those of the historians, the two groups work in an isolation that handicaps both. Keeping traditional faith with the written word, historians refuse to take advantage of the potential which the camera and film offer. Only in the past decade, as historians mastered sources other than the written word — the interview technique and statistics for example — and witnessed the diminishing enrollment in history courses, have they shown more willingness to experiment with film. However, suspicions that the film provides only entertainment cause many still to hesitate to incorporate it into their research and teaching and accord it the scholarly legitimacy it deserves. There seems to be a generation correlation in respect to receptivity of film: the younger the scholars the more at ease they seem to be with the medium and the more willing to incorporate it. Perhaps they more fully appreciate that the new generations of students enrolling in the universities are image oriented. In 1967, for example, the *New York Times* reported that the average student graduating from high school had spent 15,000 hours viewing television and concluded, "Their psychological intake system is programmed for

---

[5] Annette Michelson, "The Man with the Movie Camera," *Artform* (March, 1972), p. 62.

A Filmic Approach to Latin America's Past

the moving image."[6] It was a conclusion widely popularized by Marshall McLuhan.

Even if the individual historian evinces a willingness to experiment with film, he soon learns that no fixed methodology exists for its use — quite a contrast to the elaborate rules established to employ written documents. Hence, he faces the challenge of learning how to use the film as source material and evidence for understanding and explaining the past. Often uncertain of how to incorporate the film in class, he either avoids it altogether or haphazardly selects a film, which may or may not be worthwhile, and projects it without integrating it into the lectures. It is little wonder, then, that most students have come to regard the film as a respite from study, a welcome opportunity to stop taking notes and perhaps even to stop thinking. By these methods, historians encourage the concept of film solely as entertainment.

Those reluctant to use film raise a series of arguments to oppose it. The most recurrent one finds film too subjective. It is an unfair argument. Of course films are subjective, but, then, too, so are books. Yet, accustomed to working with words, historians no longer seem overly exercised about their subjectivity. Indeed, books and films share a surprising number of similarities. In fact, I would counter most arguments hurled against the film by first questioning whether they cannot apply as well to written documents.

Naturally, significant differences also exist between films and books, but many of those differences are mechanical: a book can be read slowly, at leisure, and then reread, whereas once the film starts it should not be stopped until it finishes and it is difficult to return to one shot or sequence; viewing a movie means most of the note-taking and reflection follow rather than accompany the film; books are readily available in libraries and bookstores, while films are expensive (even for rental) and require costly equipment to project them. Yet, it behooves historians to accustom themselves to the new medium. As they do so the trend would be for films to become more readily available and easier to handle. Equipment becomes less complex and easier to operate. Experts report that

---

[6] July 2, 1967.

the day of the cartridge film is upon us, an advance that will lower the cost of film, make it more available, and reduce technical problems of viewing. Obviously the films still do not carry the usual scholarly accouterments of footnotes, bibliographies, and statistical tables, but there is no reason why the closing footage of a film could not list its sources. An alternative would be to accompany the film with a printed pamphlet listing the sources and indicating how the film was made.

Film does possess a "language" of its own, and those initiating themselves into its use will have to master it, neither an unpleasant nor a difficult task. Dozens of books offer a verbal introduction to the language of film, but none of them surpasses the unique visual introduction to the subject recently prepared by the McGraw-Hill Book Company. With a package of thirteen short films, the *Contemporary Films' Mini Course on Film Study* provides just about all the scholar or student needs to understand filmic communication.

Unlike the written word, the film plays on two senses at once: the eye and the ear. A book describes reality through abstract symbols; the film uses direct images of reality: it shows reality. Thus, the historian should note that in at least this respect the film could be less subjective than the written word since it transfers the image directly to the mind rather than requiring, as the written description does, the mind to create an image, one that naturally varies with each person. Thus, film leaves less to the imagination, requiring perhaps less interpretation than other forms of communication.

In the final analysis, we must recognize that the film will not supply exactly the same information that may be extracted from conventional written sources. It does not convey statistical and conceptual data as written words and symbols. Still, we must bear in mind that it is not meant to supplant the written word. Rather, film and the written word should complement each other. Together they can deepen our perception of the past, so much so that we can conclude that no research into a twentieth-century topic could be considered complete until the film archives have been searched for relevant reels.

The fundamental premise for the use of film as history is based on the acceptance of the idea that filmmakers can interpret society and its past (or specious present) as accurately and as validly as other intellectuals can. Of course historians should not expect — nor require — filmmakers to fit into their traditional molds. They must realize that filmmakers may introduce new methods or approaches to the study of the past. Roberto Rossellini, certainly one of the foremost filmmaker-historians, defines his historiographical position as follows: "We must learn history in its build-up and not in dates, names, alliances, betrayals, wars, and conquests, but following instead the thread of the transformation of thought."[7] On the other hand, there is no reason for the historian not to become a filmmaker and bring to the camera his own historiographical skills.

Over the last three-quarters of a century, filmmakers have shot millions of feet of film. Captured on celluloid are the most momentous events as well as the most mundane. Some of the filmmakers were fully conscious that they were recording historic events for posterity; others were oblivious to the potential historical value of their work. Consciously or unconsciously they visually preserved the past.

Film, any film, provides a unique visual perspective of the past. The question arises as to how the historian can make proper use of it. At random, I consulted six basic guides used to train aspiring historians in the tools of their profession. Only one mentioned — in six words — the possibility of using film; none provided any hints as to how it might be done. A methodological approach to the scholarly use of film begs discussion.

Because documentary film can be particularly useful to the historian, let me confine my discussion to that genre. What is said can be applied, with some modification, to other forms of film as well. The examples I select pertain to Latin America, the area I know best.

The documentary film records the time in which it was made as well as the time about which it was made. It is both a recorder and reflector and has historical value on both levels. It shows *visually* people and events as they were in time. Miraculously moving before one's very eyes are the people of the past with all the

---

[7] Quoted in *Cinéaste,* Vol. VI, No. 2, p. 5 n. 3.

accouterments and artifacts of their lives. The film catches them snuggly fitted into their geographic and social environments. It permits the viewer to witness the past in all its detail and to a large extent thereby to understand the past better.

In 1944, the March of Time produced *Brazil*[8] to introduce Americans to their wartime ally. It was part of an extensive program encouraged, and partly financed, by the U.S. government to acquaint Americans with their neighbors in this hemisphere at a time when they seemed extremely important to our security.[9] When produced and shown, *Brazil* was a current events documentary, showing what was happening in that South American nation at that moment and revealing attitudes in the United States toward and about it. Now, three decades later, it serves as a fascinating document of the mid-1940s showing much about the Brazil and the United States of that period. It contains, among many things, some valuable footage of President Getúlio Vargas accepting the homage of the urban masses and interacting with generals, politicians, and diplomats. Those scenes offer succeeding generations of historians the remarkable opportunity of seeing Vargas in action and the visual revelations appreciably increase the perception of the populist leader. It is one thing to read a description of Vargas; it is another to see a photograph of him; but the personage takes on added depth when we can watch him in action decades after his death, something only film can realize. The phenomenon of Peronismo becomes likewise easier to understand and explain after viewing the magnetic interaction between Juan Perón and the masses. The collage of newsreel clips composing the documentary *Perón and Evita*[10] offers that opportunity. The hundreds of thousands of cheering people

---

[8] If the text does not reveal the date the film was made or the filmmaker, I give the information in a footnote, provided it is available to me. The footnote indicates where the film I consulted is located. *Brazil,* for example, is located in the UCLA Media Library, Los Angeles 90024. Its number is 3724.

[9] Walter Wanger, "Film Phenomena: The Film World Looks to Latin America," *Saturday Review of Literature,* Vol. XXXI, No. 16 (April 17, 1943), p. 42.

[10] Produced by CBS-TV News, "Twentieth Century Series," 1958; UCLA Media Library, No. 10664.

greeting Juan Perón, the obvious devotion of the multitudes to Eva Perón reject the facile descriptions of the Peróns as corrupt, self-serving despots which have been the standard treatment accorded them by a majority of the international press. In short, the visual images do not corroborate the written word, and the apparent contradiction rightly gives pause, impelling historians who rely exclusively on the written medium to weight their conclusions further. In this particular case, film cautions the historian that the written word can be monopolized by those subscribing to similar views. So, too, can the film, but <u>frequently the camera captures enough in its sweep to present at least some</u> of the <u>contradictions</u>.

In that respect, film can preserve aspects of a society which are less written about. <u>The documentary does more than illustrate political events</u> and focus on the lives of the great. <u>The camera's inquiring eye often takes in the life-styles of the humble</u> by revealing myriad details about their dress, behavior, interaction, and so on. Potentially film can serve as a major tool for the study of social history. The anthropologists have proved much quicker than the historians to adopt the film as the best method of recording the life-styles of people. John Collier's book, *Visual Anthropology*, is a practical guide to the methodology of using photographs and films to study people, and it is orienting new generations of anthropologists.

Students of Latin America's past have never fully portrayed life-styles. Films can assist them in doing so. <u>*Young Uruguay*</u>[11] and <u>*Montevideo Family*</u>,[12] for example, depict the urban middle class in the mid-1940s, demonstrating the strong "international flavor" of its life-style. On the other hand, <u>*Brazil: The Gathering Millions*</u>[13] plunges the viewer into the *favelas* of Rio de Janeiro in the mid 1960s to reveal the living conditions and habits of a large segment of that city's impoverished population, an effective

---

[11] Produced by United World Films, 1943; UCLA Media Library, No. 3462.

[12] Directed by Julien Bryan, 1949; UCLA Media Library, No. 3403.

[13] Produced by NET "Population Problem Series," 1967; UCLA Media Library, No. 6611.

pictorial essay on the overwhelming problems of housing, sanitation, nutrition, unemployment, and illiteracy confronting Latin America. The social realism that commends these films can turn to romanticism through the camera of filmmakers who eschew reality to convey the message of "poor but happy." Films like books vary in quality and viewpoint, and the scholar and student must use equal care in selecting those of substance. Social historians will be rewarded for their efforts, however. The film provides a type of visual detail and data unavailable elsewhere.

The picture provides more than descriptive detail. A judicial juxtaposition of scenes, one of the most effective elements of the language of films, can create a powerful visual essay. Two such examples were made by the brilliant American documentary filmmaker Julien Bryan in the 1940s: _Good Neighbor Family_[14] and _High Plain_.[15] The latter fascinates by showing in 1949 in Bolivia the existence of the neofeudal estate, only slightly modified by the centuries. The Indian serfs approach their patron, kneel down, and kiss his hand. In the evening, a majordomo sings out the work tasks for the next day, while Indians listen attentively in the shadowed doorways of their huts. The camera follows the Indians as they till the land, three days for themselves, three days for the patron. They work hard, but the lack of proper tools foretells the continued inefficient exploitation of the land. *Good Neighbor Family* is probably the best essay, written or filmed, on the basic Latin American institution: the family. Scenes varying from the homes of the most powerful elites to the humblest working class dwellings illustrate the strong family fiber. Further, the film makes a point that sociologists did not grasp until two decades later: families migrating from the countryside to the city stay together although the urban environment forces them to adapt to some changes. Raymundo Glazyer, the Argentine documentary filmmaker, also has shown himself master of the

---

[14] Directed by Julien Bryan, 1943; UCLA Media Library No. 3413.

[15] Directed by Julien Bryan, 1949; UCLA Media Library No. 3466.

filmic essay. His <u>The Land Burns</u>[16] studies the poverty of the marginal rural proletariat of Brazil's *sertão,* emphasizing their lack of control over their own destiny. His <u>Mexico: The Frozen Revolution</u>[17] is a powerful analysis of the failures of the Mexican Revolution, well filmed, well argued, and very provocative.

The documentary also deals with the significant trends of twentieth-century Latin America. The complex process of urbanization comes alive to the researcher viewing the innumerable footage shot of Latin American cities during the past seventy-five years. Films such as <u>Lima (1944),</u>[18] <u>La Paz (1949),</u>[19] <u>Belo Horizonte (1949),</u>[20] <u>São Paulo (1949)</u>[21] show major Latin American cities on the eve of a demographic explosion. In the years since those films were made, the population of La Paz more than doubled, Lima and Belo Horizonte tripled, and São Paulo quadrupled in size. Obviously the historian or sociologist of Latin America's urbanization who has viewed some of the film footage taken of the region's cities over the past decades will have a perception of the magnitude, significance, and problems of urbanization unobtainable by those whose research has been confined exclusively to the written word. The film injects life into population statistics and provides unforgettable drama to the figures of per capita income. It can bring similar depth to the study of other notable twentieth-century trends, of which industrialization and modernization would be suitable examples.

If films reflect change in Latin America, they also mirror continuity. Beneath a veneer of modernity, much of Latin America remains unaltered, very much submerged in its colonial and neocolonial past. By juxtaposing Julien Bryan's sensitive

---

[16] UCLA Media Library, No. 10609.

[17] 1970. Tricontinental Film Center, P.O. Box 4430, Berkeley, Calif. 94704.

[18] Directed by Julien Bryan, 1944; UCLA Media Library, No. 3517.

[19] Directed by Julien Bryan, 1949; UCLA Media Library, No. 3477.

[20] Produced by the United States Office of Inter-American Affairs (USOIA), 1949; UCLA Media Library, No. 3480.

[21] Produced by USOIA, 1949; No. 3481.

portrait *Bolivia* (1946)[22] with the highly informative and perceptive BBC documentary *End of a Revolution?* (1967)[23] one sees how little Bolivia has changed in the course of twenty-one years, an astonishing observation when one realizes that in that period it underwent a major revolution, one of only four in the twentieth century which have tried to transform Latin America. That revolution redistributed the land, created a new peasant class, and nationalized the major natural resource, tin. Yet, despite those momentous changes, many of the scenes from *End of a Revolution?* eerily recall those of *Bolivia.* One film presents the visual evidence of how the miners lived in 1946; the other offers pictorial insights into their living standard in 1967. Substantial similarities link the two images which the eye immediately recognizes and the mind registers without the intervening interpretation of words. The result is an impressive proof of continuity, the extent of which it is only possible to appreciate through the image.

The film provides at least a threefold impact on the viewer. The first is factual. The film is a precise record of material reality. Here is what a Mexican village looked like in 1939; here is how Indians behaved in the Chichicastenango marketplace in 1944; here is the extent of overt modernization of São Paulo in 1949; here is how Perón addressed the *descamisados* in 1952. The moving pictures show the interaction of people with each other and with their environment, while supplying such factual details as dress, articles for sale in the market, methods of land cultivation, use of the land, extent of technology, modes of transportation. The film is especially useful to introduce foreign cultures. Cheaply and efficiently the film brings into the lecture hall or study distant geography and people. It partly overcomes cultural bias or ignorance by leaping hurdles that handicap our efforts to know, appreciate, and understand another culture. With equal ease it gives the viewer ready access to a wooden shanty along the Amazon or the presidential palace in Caracas. The film possesses

---

[22] UCLA Media Library, No. 10062.

[23] Produced by Brian Moser for Granada Films; UCLA Media Library, No. 10606.

those unique qualities which easily expand the viewers' consciousness and experience by giving them direct visual contact with their subject.

The second impact of the film is emotional. The very fact that the viewer is actually witnessing the past, seeing it replayed in a dark room on a bright screen on which his eyes are forced to focus, elicits an emotional response, that is, an involvement. Appropriate music, color, shadows, light, and skillful camera work heighten that response. Careful editing will intensify it even more. In Jorge Sanjines's *Yawar Mallku* (*Blood of the Condor*) (1969),[24] for example, the intercutting of scenes of the impoverished and despairing Sixto trying to sell his only possession, a bed, to raise money to buy blood for his injured brother with scenes of marching Bolivian soldiers proudly displaying their modern— and expensive — weaponry creates in the viewer a series of strong emotional responses from sympathy to anger. In addition, such cutting raises all sorts of questions about national goals, foreign aid, and "development." Perhaps here we encounter one area of caution with the use of film either as a teaching or research device: it is capable of arousing more emotion than the written document. Emotion, however, should not be regarded negatively. The psychotherapist Alexander Lawen has pointed out, "Of the two ingredients in behavior, feeling is more important than knowledge. But our whole educational system is geared to knowledge and the denial of feeling."[25] One notable strength of the film is that it can convey both feeling and knowledge.

Added to the factual and emotional impacts of the film is the particular interpretation it offers the viewer. For each person will leave the film with an impression, conclusion, or interpretation. The documentary does not only explore reality, it expresses an opinion about it and often explains it.

---

[24] For Latin American feature-length films, the original title is given. If the film is available with English subtitles, the English title is also given and used thereafter in the text. Date of production is given, if known, as well as distributor. *Blood of the Condor* is available from the Tricontinental Film Center (see n. 17, above).

[25] Quoted in Richard A. Lacey, *Seeing with Feeling: Film in the Classroom* (Philadelphia: W. B. Saunders, 1972), p. 90.

The real significance of the film is that it actually allows us to see the past. Films provide the unique dimension to research and study of visual contact with the subject.

Three basic aspects of films concern the historian as he formulates his critique of them. First, he analyzes the film's treatment of reality, raising a series of questions such as what are the realities to which this film addresses itself; does it convincingly depict them; what depth of reality does it provide; can the filmmaker's concept of reality be accepted; and does his version of reality correspond or clash with reality as the viewer conceives it or is aware of it? Second, the historian wants to understand the various levels of meaning – factual, emotional, and interpretive – of the film. Here the historian must extract meaning from images, a challenge since his training heretofore has been to interpret words. At its simplest, a film can be just an arrangement of a series of images, each with its own significance and meaning. Few films are that elementary. Most require intellectual involvement, an intense, active participation from the viewer who relates the images to one another, to his own experience, and to the narration and/or dialogue in an effort to understand the objective, impact, meaning, purpose, and significance of the film. Finally each viewer must assess the value of the film for himself. Reflecting a variety of experiences, each viewer will assign different values, or no value, to the film. As the historian's skill in using the image develops, he will be extracting data on various levels. Then, perhaps, he will appreciate Carl Sandburg's wry observation: all movies good or bad are educational and Hollywood is a more effective educational institution than Harvard.

2

The documentary film comes in several varieties; one of the most exciting is the so-called <u>fictional</u>, a genre increasingly cultivated by talented young Latin American filmmakers. Actually the fictional and nonfictional <u>documentaries</u> share much in common. Both are concerned with reality; both interpret reality; both treat it creatively and imaginatively. A major difference lies in where and for what purpose the filmmaker applies imagination. In the nonfictional documentary, imagination is used in the technique of presentation, whereas the fictional relates something imaginary or semi-imaginary. It takes some license with reality. Imagination is used to reconstruct situations that reflect and symbolize reality. Taking an example from another geographical area, Joan Mellen points to Gillo Pontecorvo's *The Battle of Algiers* as an outstanding example of the fictional documentary able to convey the importance – the essence – of an historical event:

> Although it cannot claim to express the actual facts, *The Battle of Algiers* saturates us with the atmosphere of truth. For the duration of the film its images substitute for real events and immerse us into one man's vision of them. What is so noteworthy about *The Battle of Algiers* is not only that we feel that we are watching a film of events as they occurred, but that Pontecorvo has achieved a supreme fiction, capturing the inner truth of the history he transforms.[26]

What she says about that film can be applied with equal force to fictional documentaries made in Latin America, such as *Ganga Zumba* (Brazil, 1963, Carlos Diegues), *Menino de Engenho* (*Plantation Boy*, Brazil, 1965, Walter Lima), *Lucia* (*Lucia*, Cuba, 1969, Humberto Solas), and *El Coraje del Pueblo* (*The Courage of the People*, Bolivia, 1971, Jorge Sanjines),[27] or made about Latin America, such as Costa-Garvas's *State of Seige* or Pontecorvo's *Burn*. All the situations depicted in such fictional documentaries may not be real, in which case they substitute for reality, but very often the events in fact did occur and the fictional documentary presents an imaginative reconstruction of them. In short, the fictional and nonfictional documentaries share a similar goal: a creative search for reality.

In the search for reality, the imaginative recreation of situations and experiences that could have happened are not unknown – or

---

[26] Joan Mellen, *Filmguide to the* Battle of Algiers (Bloomington: Indiana University Press, 1973), p. 57.

[27] *Ganga Zumba* and *Plantation Boy* are available from New Yorker Films, 43 West 61st St., New York, N.Y. 10023. *Lucia* and *The Courage of the People* are distributed by Tricontinental Film Center.

unused — by the historian. Certainly those historians who make generalizations about life-styles or multiple experiences engage in an activity similar to the fictional documentary filmmaker: the creation of the composite in which a distilled example represents a model beyond the single component. In drawing a composite set of life-styles of the Middle Ages, as A. H. de Oliveira Marques so brilliantly did in his *Daily Life in Portugal in the Late Middle Ages,* or of the adventures of covered wagons trekking westward over the plains, the historian creates a fictional example, albeit one based on innumerable, verifiable individual accounts. William Hickling Prescott, who ranks as a preeminent American historian, never shrank from imagining conversations in which he assumed the principal historical personages of his works had engaged. Both the *Conquest of Mexico* and the *Conquest of Peru* abound in them. In doing so, he merely followed the precedent of Thucydides whom most people would regard as one of the fathers of modern history. Indeed, so long as it is kept under control, historians cultivate what they call "historical imagination" as an asset to their research and writing, a better insight into the topics they study.

It is not necessary to delve very far into the historical manuals before discovering the high value historians place on "imagination." One advises the aspiring historian, "History involves the imaginative understanding of experience and its communication to an audience. It is closely related to the art of the novel, for both tell a story, the main difference lying in the amount of imaginative reconstruction of facts and personalities."[28] Perhaps Louis Gottschalk provides the best link between fictional and nonfictional, between the filmmaker and the historian, in his discussion of "verisimilitude":

> It might be well to point out again that what is meant by calling a particular credible is not that it is actually what happened, but that it is as close to what actually happened as we can learn from a critical examination of the best available sources. This means verisimilar

---

[28] Robert V. Daniels, *Studying History: How and Why* (Englewood Cliffs, N.J.: Prentice-Hall, 1966), pp. 72-73.

at a high level. It connotes something more than merely not being preposterous in itself or even than plausible and yet is short of meaning accurately descriptive of past actuality. In other words, the historian establishes verisimilitude rather than objective truth.[29]

The application of imagination to the study of the past is but one bond between historians and the makers of fictional documentaries.

Similar to historians, the makers of fictional documentaries also treat people in time and space, either the relationship of individuals to society at a given moment (always the past) or along a time continuum. Film possesses that "magic" quality of transporting the viewer visually to the era, as well as the area, in which events took place.

Causation absorbs the attention of these young filmmakers. In his *Alianza para el Progresso* (*The Alliance for Progress*),[30] Julio Luduena offers a biting explanation for Latin America's "underdevelopment." On the other hand, Nelson Pereira dos Santos provides a more subtle explanation of the political passivity of the rural proletariat in his *Vidas Secas (Barren Lives)*.[31] Glauber Rocha suggests complex and fascinating explanations for the political behavior of intellectuals in his difficult *Terra em Transe (Land in Anguish)*.[32]

If factual exposition and causation concern the filmmakers so does interpretation. Their interpretations lie not only in the script and image but comes across to the viewer through an array of filmic devices and techniques not least of which is creative editing. The filmmakers cited in this essay are masters of technique; they compare with the best anywhere. They have mastered the filmic devices that enhance their language of images and employ them in conveying their interpretation and meaning.

---

[29] Louis Gottschalk, *Understanding History: A Primer of Historical Method* (New York: Knopf, 1964), pp. 139-140.

[30] 1972, Argentina. Tricontinental Film Center.

[31] 1963, Brazil. Contemporary Films/McGraw-Hill, 1714 Stockton, San Francisco, Calif. 94133.

[32] 1966, Brazil. New Yorker Films.

Time, space, people, factual exposition, causation, and interpretation are the ingredients compounded by historians. They also are the essential components of the successful fictional documentaries being produced in contemporary Latin America. The historian and the fictional documentary filmmaker, then, on closer scrutiny, share much in common.

Many contemporary Latin American filmmakers move back and forth between fictional and nonfictional documentaries, further blurring the boundary that may separate those two filmic types. According to the director of the Cuban Film Institute, Alfredo Guevara, Cuban filmmakers are equally at home with fictional and nonfictional documentaries, considering them as "different ways to express the same reality."³³ They frequently intercut newsreel footage into their fictional documentaries. *Memorias del Subdesarrollo (Memories of Underdevelopment)*³⁴ provides the perfect example of that technique effectively used. Today's generation is just the latest wave of fictional documentary filmmakers in Latin America, although assuredly the most sophisticated to appear thus far.

The invention of the motion picture camera coincided with a rising tide of nationalism in Latin America, and the Latin Americans at once seized on the film as an appropriate means to encourage that nationalism. It offered an obvious advantage in those countries where a majority of the citizenry was illiterate.

The fledgling Mexican film industry actively promoted fictional documentaries to glorify the past. As part of the centennial celebrations in 1910, Felipe de Jesús Haro produced *El Grito de Dolores,* a patriotic hymn to Miguel Hidalgo, the hero of Mexican independence. The appearance of *Cuauhtémoc* in 1918 reflected the revived interest in Mexico's Indian past, also notable in music, literature, dance, and art. At about the same time the Ministry of War expressed an interest in filmic interpretations of the Revolution and financed such films as *Juan Soldado, El Precio de la Gloria,* and *Honor Militar.* The Revolution provided filmmakers

---

³³ Michael Myerson, *Memories of Underdevelopment: The Revolutionary Films of Cuba* (New York: Grossman, 1973), p. 26.

³⁴ 1968, Cuba. Directed by Tomas Gutierrez Alea. Tricontinental Film Center.

with a seemingly endless inspiration, sometimes with a license that obscured rather than clarified the past. A recent and highly realistic recreation of that revolutionary past is the excellent *Reed: Insurgent Mexico*,[35] which indicates the complicated rivalries and many personal sacrifices that formed the details of the monumental struggles during the second decade of this century.

Lacking such an intense nationalistic impetus as the Revolution gave Mexicans, the early Brazilian filmmakers paid only partial attention to historical themes. In 1911, Salvatore Lazzaro made the first filmic version of *O Guarany* — four other versions were produced during the following decade! — that quintessence of Brazilian nationalism. In its romantic plot, an Indian chief and the daughter of a Portuguese noble fall in love, the symbolic intertwining of the New World and the Old to create Brazil. First, as a novel, then as an opera, and, after 1911, as a movie, *O Guarany* appealed mightily to the national spirit. In fact, the overture to the opera (always played along with the film) is considered on a par with the national anthem as a major hymn to Brazilian patriotism.

Beginning in 1915, filmmakers paid greater attention to historical films, many of which, *Inocência, O Retirada da Laguna,* and *O Caçador de Esmeraldas,* for example, derived from well-known works in Brazilian literature with the same title. Doubtless the approach of Brazil's first centenary celebration of independence encouraged the new film industry to turn to historical epics. In 1918, Brazilians could watch *Tiradentes,* episodes from the life of a martyr to independence, and *O Grito do Ipiranga,* an account of events surrounding the declaration of independence. As in Mexico, the Ministry of War favored such enterprises with its cooperation and encouragement. To commemorate 150 years of independence in 1972, the government financed a lavish remake of *O Grito do Ipiranga,* retitling it *Independência ou Morte.* The Minister of Education spoke out, after its premiere, in praise of historical films. Indeed, the government evinced deep pleasure with its sesquicentennial film.

---

[35] 1972, Mexico. Directed by Paul Leduc. New Yorker Films.

Early Argentine filmmakers also adapted historical episodes to the screen. The first fictional films, *El Fusilamiento de Dorrego, La Batalla de San Lorenzo*, and *Juan Moreira*, all made by Mario Gallo, found their inspiration in national history. *Nobleza Gaucha*, produced in 1915 by Eduardo Martínez and Ernesto Gunche, romanticized the brave gaucho of the pampa, a figure who thereafter recurred constantly on the screen. Through film and literature the gaucho took on the symbolism of Argentine nationalism. A Chilean film industry developed more slowly, but it too followed patterns set elsewhere in Latin America. In 1925, Pedro Sienna filmed *El Húsar de la Muerte*, a major production about Chile's independence period.

Viewing these fictional treatments of historical themes, some general characteristics stand out. First, nationalism motivated their production, and consequently an obsequious glorification of the "fatherland" predominates. Second, the films do not pretend to question any basic institutions. Quite the contrary, they confirm the wisdom of the nation's heroes and the institutions they implanted or supported. Third, the films by and large take an elitist viewpoint lauding the individual or hero. With rare exception does the emphasis fall on the role of the people in history. In this respect, the films follow well-established Latin American historiographical dicta. As the Brazilian historian of the nineteenth century, the Visconde de Pôrto Alegre, expressed it: "To know the history of any period it is necessary to know the biographies of all the outstanding men of the time." Such elitist concepts by no means disappeared from twentieth-century historiography as the Peruvian historian Francisco García Calderón testifies: "The history of the South American Republics may be reduced to the biographies of the representative men." Further, most of those historical recreations concentrated on a narrative line giving scant attention to causation.

The difference between those historical epics and the recent fictional documentaries is enormous. The new generation of filmmakers stresses social realism, the role of the people, and causation. Interweaving art and politics, these filmmakers tell us something is grossly wrong in Latin American society. Their films visualize, analyze, discuss, and illustrate pressing social, economic, and political problems and sometimes provide or suggest possible solutions to them. Their heroes are the little people who struggle against the oppression of the iniquitous institutions. The Chilean filmmaker Miguel Littin so convincingly demonstrates the injustice of those institutions to the rural masses in his *El Chacal de Nahueltoro* (*The Jackal of Nahueltoro*)[36] that death seems preferable, at least to the leading character, to continued misery. As that film also illustrates, these filmmakers study the relationship of the individual to his society at a given moment and then go on to explain that relationship. They identify closely with the plight of the people their films depict. Obviously angered by the injustices of their society and sincerely committed to social change, they use their cameras as weapons of combat. Defining the fictional documentary in her important essay, included in Chapter II, Professor Joan Mellen concludes, "The *raison d'etre* of the fictional documentary is the search for clarity about historical issues which affect us far beyond the two hour microcosm enacted on the film."[37] Entertainment is not the objective of these dedicated filmmakers. Their work is political, their films reflect the crosscurrents of societies in conflict between change and the changeless.[38]

The young Latin American cineastes who appear after the mid-1950s show a marked enthusiasm to reconstruct and reinterpret the past in their films, some of the finest of the fictional documentaries. Consciously aware of the relationship between their work and history, their films are significant documents of history. Their cameras are microscopes examining their own societies. The results are a wealth of filmic interpretive studies which document the frustrations, discontent, pride, hopes, and longing for change characteristic of much of contemporary Latin America.

---

[36] 1969, Chile. Tricontinental Film Center.

[37] Joan Mellen, "Film and Style: The Fictional Documentary," *Antioch Review*, Vol. 32 (1973), No. 3, p. 417 (see p. 84 above).

[38] For a broader study of this theme see Leif Furhammar and Folke Isaksson, *Politics and Film* (New York: Praeger, 1971).

Two indigenous cinema movements, one in Brazil, the other in Cuba, emerged by the close of the 1950s. Concentrating on social problems, Brazil's Cinema Nôvo looked sharply into the two areas of greatest poverty and social injustice: the *favela* (slum) and the *sertão* (the arid backlands).[39] Carlos Diegues studies the drama of the poor in the city in his *Grande Cidade* (*The Big City,* 1966),[40] emphasizing its brutalization of the rural migrant, who, full of hope, came to the city only to be plunged into conditions worse than those he fled. Doubtless still the masterpiece of the Cinema Nôvo is *Barren Lives,* directed by Nelson Pereira dos Santos. He brilliantly transferred to screen the powerful novel of the same name. Rural poverty, dependency, and underdevelopment are depicted with unflinching accuracy in this extraordinary document on how an impoverished family survives in the backlands of Brazil. Of the many young directors at work in the Cinema Nôvo movement in the 1960s, Glauber Rocha stands out as the most productive and imaginative. He remains concerned with Brazilian reality but increasingly has imposed a heavy symbolism on his films. Possibly still the best of Rocha's growing output is *Deus e o Diablo na Terra do Sol* (*Black God, White Devil,* 1963),[41] which introduces the viewer to the principal human types found in the *sertão*: the peasant, cowboy, rancher, landowner, and religious mystic. His later *Antônio das Mortes,* an operatic drama of epic proportions, includes, besides those types, the *cangaceiro* (backland bandit) and the intellectual in a film of complex political and

---

[39] The bibliography on the Cinema Nôvo is growing. As representative studies see Alex Viany, Nelson Pereira dos Santos, and Glauber Rocha, "Cinema Nôvo: Origens, Ambições e Perspectivas," *Revista Civilização Brasileira,* No. 1 (March, 1965), pp. 185-196; Glauber Rocha, *Revisão Crítica do Cinema Brasileiro* (Rio de Janeiro: Editora Civilização Brasileira, 1963); "Cinema Nôvo vs. Cultural Colonialism: An Interview with Glauber Rocha," *Cinéaste,* Vol. IV, No. 1 (Summer, 1970), pp. 2-9; Jacques Belmans, "Critique et Réalité Sociales dans le Cinema Nôvo," *Études Cinématographiques,* Nos. 93-96 (Paris: Lettres Modernes, 1972), pp. 41-60; Luis Quesada, "Brazil's Film-Makers Move to the City: The Force of Realism," *Atlas,* September, 1971, pp. 51-52; Glauber Rocha, "Cabezas Cortadas: Interview with Glauber Rocha," *Afterimage,* No. 3 (Summer, 1971), pp. 68-77; *idem.,* " 'We Are the Harbingers of Revolution': An Interview with Glauber Rocha," *Atlas,* October, 1971, pp. 54-55.

[40] New Yorker Films.

[41] *Ibid.*

mystical dimensions. By the time he made *Antônio,* the rigid military censorship in Brazil had forced Rocha to adopt intricate symbolism, so much so that the film speaks principally to intellectuals. Unsympathetic to the purposes of the Cinema Nôvo, the military rulers strangled it and returned the film industry to the innocuous domain of the soap opera and musicals by the end of the 1960s. Obviously they frowned upon the film's exposure of truth for the masses to see, preferring a lulling dream world to reality.

Nurtured by Fidel Castro after his advent to power in 1959, the Cuban cinema blossomed into one of the most alluring cinemagraphic flowers in Latin America. The Cuban Film Institute (Instituto Cubano del Arte e Industria Cinematográficos) was established March 24, 1959, and has since produced over 300 documentaries and 50 feature-length films. Much of the Cuban filmmakers' attention focused on interpreting their country's past. In his alternatingly lyric and realistic *Lucia,* Humberto Solas studied the woman's role in three Cuban struggles which have shaped the history of modern Cuba: the war for independence in 1895, the fight to overthrow the Machado regime in 1932, and the literacy campaign of the 1960s. In another effective look at the past, Manuel Octavio Gómez recreated in his *La Primera Carga al Machete* events from the guerrilla warfare against Spain in 1895, using the technique of the on-the-spot cameraman to simulate newsreel reporting. He links his roles as filmmaker and historian. He observed,

> I thought it would be interesting to deal with a historical event as if it were happening today, or, better, as seen through the eyes of a person who would have been there as events were taking place. It wasn't simply a formal intention, but a conceptual desire to make history more alive, more urgent. The style of the traditional historical film bothers me a great deal because I always find it rather museum-like, lifeless.[42]

Thus far, the Cuban film most accessible to audiences in the United States is *Memories of Underdevelopment,* a witty and

---

[42] Quoted in Myerson, *Memories of Underdevelopment,* p. 170.

penetrating analysis of attitudes of the former bourgeoisie toward revolution. Its director, Tomas Gutierrez Alea, like his contemporaries, regards his films as useful historical documents. He classifies his *Una Pelea contra los Demonios* as an exploration of the historical roots of Cuba: "It is an effort to examine our most obscure past, of seeing in a new light our beginnings, still so little examined by history, of becoming conscious of our roots."[43]

By the middle of the 1960s, the movements pioneered and invigorated by the Brazilians and Cubans had spread to other parts of Latin America. Some young, determined, and talented directors in Argentina, Bolivia, and Chile produced films reflective of their national environments, past, and problems. To make their films, they struggled against every possible obstacle: lack of financing, limited and poor equipment, scanty technical facilities, and always without the sympathy of a distribution system dominated by Hollywood. Often government hostility further hindered their efforts.

Perhaps the experience of the Bolivian filmmakers, grouped together informally as a production unit known as Ukamau, represents the extreme in working under handicaps.[44] Their film budgets never exceed $50,000. They receive no governmental subventions. Quite the opposite they have been the focal point of much governmental harassment. They have only one camera at their disposal and most of the processing of the films must be done outside the country. Approximately 350,000 people saw their film *Blood of the Condor,* considered to be a huge audience for a film in impoverished Bolivia. No one receives a salary. Their work is done out of conviction, avocation, and love. Despite such obstacles, Ukamau produced four outstanding films from 1966 to 1974.[45]

---

[43] Tomas Gutierrez Alea, "Presentación de una Pelea Cubana contra los Demonios," *Cine Cubano,* Nos. 78/79/80, p. 49.

[44] Information in this paragraph comes from interviews with two leading members of Ukamau, Antonio Eguino and Oscar Soria, in La Paz, August 28, 29, 1973.

[45] The young Bolivian filmmakers like their counterparts elsewhere in Latin America put their emphasis on the impact rather than on the technicalities of the film. For example, the Argentine filmmaker Fernando Solanas has remarked, "The important thing was not the film itself but that which the film provoked" ("Cinema as a Gun: An Interview with Fernando Solanas," *Cinéaste,* Vol. III, No. 2 [Fall, 1969], p. 20).

Jorge Sanjines, a member of Ukamau, although for several years now forced to live in exile, is perhaps one of the most interesting of the current Latin American directors. He is certainly one of the most articulate. Realism absorbs him; so does history. In fact, Sanjines sees one of his primary duties as the rescue from oblivion of the historical events in which the people participated. In filming a massacre of striking Bolivian tin miners by government troops in 1967 for his film *El Coraje del Pueblo* (translated as either *The Courage of the People* or *The Night of San Juan*), Sanjines gathered together the survivors as well as some of the original troops to create the event for the camera in as perfect a detail as was possible.[46] The recreation of the event — and its preservation as history by the camera (the only other known recorded account of what happened appeared in the newspapers of distant La Paz written by journalists who witnessed neither the strike nor the massacre) — satisfied Sanjines as accurate. He commented:

> We felt that we were working alongside the people in a project that meant a lot to everyone who participated, and we felt that the people were as clearly conscious of all of that as we ourselves were, since they continually demanded of us the greatest authenticity with relation of the events, places, persons, and situations reconstructed. But not only were they demanding of others, but they in turn demanded much of themselves and it was that exacting attitude which inspired our own effort.[47]

The Courage of the People is the third film in which Sanjines has concentrated on Bolivian historical events.

A leitmotiv of his films is an analysis of the relations between Indians and whites (or the "Europeanized"). Owing to the very nature of the country, its population and history, all Bolivian intellectuals have concentrated on that theme but none as effectively or provocatively as the Ukamau group. What makes these films even more fascinating is that they are directed to the Indians themselves and facilitate discussion and dialogue with

---

[46] 1971, Bolivia. Tricontinental Films. "The Courage of the People: An Interview with Jorge Sanjines," *Cinéaste,* Vol. V, No. 2 (Spring, 1972), pp. 18-20.

[47] *Ibid.,* p. 19.

them about Bolivia, its problems, promise, and potential. The other intellectuals use the printed word, suitable for discussion with other intellectuals or the literate elite, but beyond the reach of the illiterate Indian masses. Thus, through the film, Sanjines brings a study of history to wider audiences than any author could hope to reach in Bolivia.

A popular and powerful Sanjines film available in the United States is *Blood of the Condor* depicting the exploitation of the impoverished Indian masses of Bolivia, explaining some of the causes of it, and suggesting a solution: revolution. It would be difficult to find a film − or for that matter a book − which treats with greater realism and precision the problems of exploitation, dependency, and underdevelopment in Latin America. As such, *Blood of the Condor* is a powerful document of great use to the historian of Latin America or to any social scientist.

During the early 1970s, Chile Films exhibited a similar concern with history. In fact, one of its primary goals was to recapture and reinterpret Chile's past.[48] The formation of the University Film Society in 1960 gave impetus to serious filmic concern with the past. In 1961, Sergio Bravo made *La Marcha del Carbón* to document an important coal strike during the Alessandri regime, a foretaste of later concentration on recreating the past on film. The inauguration of President Salvador Allende and his Popular Unity government in 1970 brought new life to the practically moribund Chile Films. To direct Chile Films, Allende appointed Miguel Littin, whose credits included the remarkably sensitive *The Jackal of Nahueltoro*, a reconstruction of a brutal multiple slaying in southern Chile for which Littin placed the blame on the iniquitous national institutions that spawn frustration, alcoholism, and violence among the poor. He wanted his film "to denounce a decaying official state − a social decay." In speaking about how he prepared the script for this film, Littin reveals the close similarity a filmmaker can have with the historians: "I researched all available records of the case − public, journalistic, and legal. I

---

[48] Hans Ehrmann, "Cine: La era de los próceres," *Quinta Rueda,* October, 1972, p. 11.

interviewed people who were with this man in prison; I visited the places where he spent his childhood, adolescence and later life."[49]

Taking charge of Chile Films in 1970, Littin declared it first would concentrate on two goals: (1) to explain how contemporary Chilean society is the product of "hundreds of years of colonialism and dependency," and (2) to indicate how society could be transformed. Chile Films had scarcely three years to work toward those goals. One of the first actions of the military chiefs who violently ended the democratic government of President Allende on September 11, 1973, was to destroy the film industry. All the leading directors either fled or were imprisoned. One, Eduardo Paredes, was killed. The military entered the University of Chile Film Department and destroyed all the equipment. The military junta forbid the showing of films made by Chile Films, thus opening the market to Hollywood and renewed cultural domination. The Chilean screens once again reflected the dream world, fantasies, and cultural tastes of foreigners. The *Los Angeles Times* jubilantly noted under the banner "Chile Filmgoers Get a Break":

> The junta reduced Chile Films to the status of local producer of short subjects and newsreels and asked Americans to resume sending their products to Chile.
> Seven distributors with offices here airfreighted two features each. These included Paramount's "Play It Again, Sam," Universal's "The Andromeda Strain," Warner Bros. "The Cowboys," 20th Century-Fox's "Escape from the Planet of the Apes," Columbia's "The Horseman," Universal's "Chato's Land" and MGM's "The Boyfriend."[50]

Gone — at least temporarily — were the filmic studies of Chilean society and problems, films made by Chileans in the Chilean environment about Chile.

Certainly one of the characteristics of the new wave of filmmakers which makes them anathema to the traditional ruling elite is their advocacy of bold solutions to hoary and nagging problems of underdevelopment which have bedeviled Latin

---

[49] "Film in Chile: An Interview with Miguel Littin," *Cinéaste,* Vol. IV, No. 4 (Spring, 1971), p. 4.

[50] November 24, 1973.

America for half a millennium. Many of these filmmakers believe that they should not only depict reality but also attempt to explain and suggest ways of altering that reality. Those explanations seldom flatter the elite since the blame is placed at their feet, as well as on imperialism and the dependency it perpetuates. The solutions they suggest positively frighten the elite. The Indians raising their rifles to the sky in the final scene of Sanjines's *Blood of the Condor* is heady stuff. The tossing back at the police of a canister of tear gas they have just lobbed into the crowd in the closing scene of Aldo Francia's *Ya Basta Con Rezar* (Chile, 1971) is such an obvious and emotional appeal to open defiance of established authority of the pre-Allende type in Chile and to activism that it could not go unchallenged by the elites.

To alter reality, to solve Latin America's problems requires considerable knowledge of present conditions and their cause, in short a self-knowledge and self-awareness. Therefore, the new generation of filmmakers cram their films with information on history, politics, and economics. They discuss at length on celluloid the causes and consequences of underdevelopment and dependency, interrelated problems plaguing Latin America.

To be effective, according to Miguel Littin, the film must dissect and criticize society first and then propose changes. The observations of other young directors of these films of social realism convey the goals they pursue. The Argentine, Raymundo Gleyzer, advises, "It is important for a filmmaker to go to the people, to question them and then record their answers for the whole world to know. Perhaps in that way we can break the magic circle by which the oligarchies hope to sustain a fairy tale image of our people."[51] Fernando Solanas, one of the Argentine filmmakers who directed *La Hora de los Hornos* (*The Hour of the Furnaces*)[52] saw an intimate connection between the people in the film and the audience viewing it: the ordinary people came to realize that they were actors in history too. He wanted to make

---

[51] "Argentine Censorship. Protest Films . . . But for Export Only," *Atlas* (October, 1971), p. 55.

[52] 1966/1967, Argentina; Tricontinental Film Center.

A Filmic Approach to Latin America's Past

the people aware of their role and inspire them to take action, to shape their future. He seeks "a cinema of liberation and for liberation, an historic cinema of political-ideological argument."[53] Speaking frankly of the role he envisages for the filmmaker, Glauber Rocha observed, "Latin America is being shaken by a revolution, and for some of us the cinema is a political arena.... We feel we are the harbingers of the revolution that must inevitably come to Latin America."[54] Jorge Sanjines tersely commented, "Revolutionary cinema does not tell stories; it is a cinema which makes history."[55] The examination of the past inescapably becomes an integral part of the new films being produced in Latin America. In short, the filmmakers have become historians. It now remains for historians to recognize them as such and to join forces with them in the filmic approach to Latin America's past.

---

[53] "Cinema as a Gun," p. 21.

[54] " 'We Are the Harbingers of Revolution,' " p. 55.

[55] David Wilson, "Venceremos: Aspects of Latin American Political Cinema," *Sight and Sound*, Vol. XVI, No. 3 (Summer, 1972), p. 131.

Plate 1. Turning to national themes, Brazilian filmmakers focused increasing attention on the *cangaceiros* of the backlands after 1960. The scenes are from two *cangaço* films: *Corisco, O Diabo Louro* and *A Compadecida*.

Plate 2. The harsh *sertão* and the distinctive dress of the *cangaceiros* provide endless varieties for dramatic scenes.

Plate 3. In 1962, the Brazilian entry in the Cannes Film Festival, *Pagador de Promessas,* directed by Anselmo Duarte, won the Golden Palm as the best film. The victory brought international attention to the fledgling Cinema Nôvo movement which was revolutionizing the Brazilian cinema.

Plate 4. Nelson Pereira dos Santos's *Vidas Sêcas* (1963) ranks as one of the masterpieces of the Cinema Nôvo movement.

Plate 5. Nelson Xavier as Mario in *Os Fuzis,* directed by Ruy Guerra. This powerful Brazilian film treats the complex phenomenon of the "primitive rebels," the relationship of millenarianism and revolution, a subject little discussed in Latin American history.

Plate 6. Walter Lima Jr.'s *Menino de Engenho* bucolically portrays life on a decaying sugar plantation in Brazil's Northeast during the early decades of the twentieth century.

Plate 7. Leading contributors to the new Bolivian cinema movement, from left, Antonio Eguino, Oscar Soria, Jorge Sanjines.

Plate 8. The sensitive camera work of Antonio Eguino captures the rugged beauty of the Andes in *Yawar Mallku.*

Plate 9. Yawar Mallku, directed by Jorge Sanjines, is a provocative filmic study of the Indian in Bolivian society.

Plate 10. The Chilean filmmakers Miguel Littin, Héctor Ríos, and Fernando Bellet at work on the film *El Chacal de Nahueltoro.*

Plate 11. Scenes from *El Chacal de Nahueltoro.* The sensitive direction of Miguel Littin, the simplicity of the acting, and the tragedy of the story combine to make it an impressive film of social realism.

Plate 12. Alfred Guevara is director of the Instituto Cubano del Arte e Industria Cinematograficos.

Plate 13. Scenes from the epic Cuban film *Lucia*, directed by Humberto Solás in 1968. In three episodes the film depicts the role of women in Cuban history.

Plate 14. An example of Cuban cinema poster art.

Plate 15. Luis Buñuel focused on urban poverty in his dramatic Mexican film *Los Olvidados* (1951).

Plate 16. The young Pedro is trapped and destroyed by his environment in Buñel's indictment of the institutions of Latin America which perpetuate poverty.

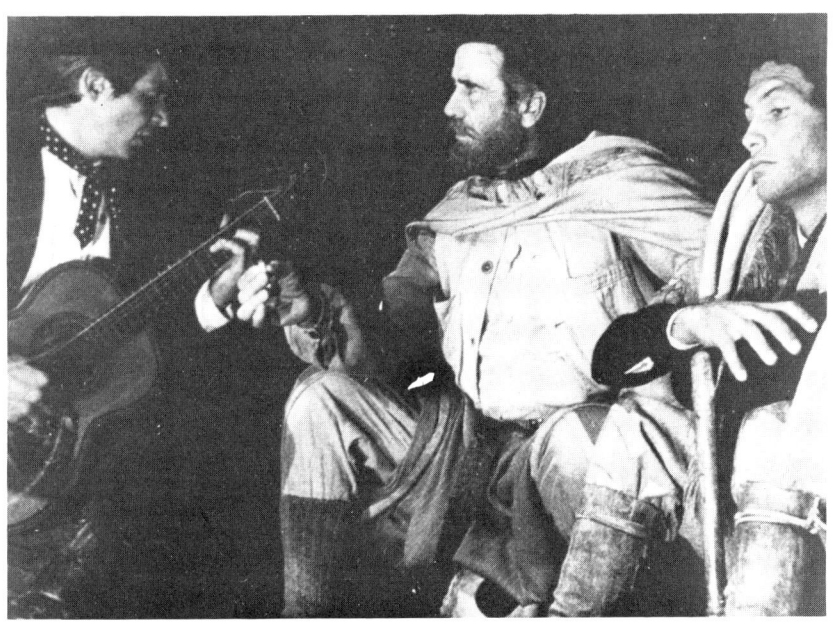

Plate 17. Don Segundo Sombra, a film made in 1969 by Manuel Antín from the *gaucho* classic by Ricardo Güiraldes, accurately documents life on the broad Argentine pampas in the early twentieth century. The film also is a fine study of Argentine character.

Plate 18. Martín Fierro, directed by Leopoldo Torre Nilsson, was voted the best Argentine film of 1969. Based on the classic poem by José Hernández, this film, too, is an essay studying Argentine character.

2

On the Theory of Film as History

Useful essays linking film and history are rare. Those by Eugene C. McCreary and Joan Mellen which follow in my opinion rank among the best. They are keys that can open doors to future studies.

McCreary, whose essay is the more general of the two, addresses his remarks to films of all types and rightly emphasizes the importance of the film as a means of communication, perhaps the most important means today. The film can be a catalyst of action. It influences those who view it and thus becomes a potent social force, propelling change or advocating stability. The new Latin American filmmakers subscribe to that belief. The film's importance to the historian, McCreary points out, derives from its unsurpassed ability to report in great visual detail about an area, period, and subject; further, it reflects the times in which it was made as well as the views of the people who made it.

Mellen's meaty discussion focuses on a very special, and very important, type of film, the fictional documentary. She reveals throughout the essay that the most successful makers of that genre employ methods that should impress the historian as sound, indeed familiar. They constitute part of the historian's methodology as well. For example, the maker of a successful fictional documentary devotes considerable effort to interviewing those who participated in the events the film will depict. A further nexus between filmmaker and historians is the search for causation. What Professor Mellen has to say about the fictional documentary, using a handful of European films as the basis for her discussion, applies perfectly to the young filmmakers who emerged in Latin America during the 1960s. From her discussion, a conceptualization for the use of the fictional documentary emerges.

Film and History:
Some Thoughts on Their Interrelationship

EUGENE C. McCREARY

It is time that historians began to exploit the potential of film in both their research and teaching activities. It has become a truism to assert that ours is an increasingly visual world, that the image as an instrument of communication has grown considerably in importance relative to the written word. Should not the historian pay greater attention to what the image can convey to him about man and his past? The present student generation, the first to reach maturity in a cultural environment where television — and thus the visual image — has served as a principal source of information and entertainment,[1] has been named "The Film Generation."[2] The openness and sensitivity of this generation to the visual image, the naturalness with which it discusses films, its awareness of the film as a valid and exciting form of expression is striking. Can the historian as a teacher afford to ignore or even to fail sufficiently to use a medium that his students find so stimulating?

The film is simultaneously an art form, an industry, and a medium of mass entertainment and mass communications. As an art form it seeks with varying success to give form to human experience, to communicate it, and to do both in such a way as to arouse in the spectator a pleasing esthetic emotion. It is as art that cinema reflects the culture in which it has been produced. And it is as art that it cannot be ignored as a source or a subject of study

---

*From *Societas,* II (Winter, 1971), pp. 51-66. Reprinted by permission of the publisher.

[1] John M. Culkin, SJ, *New York Times,* Sunday, July 2, 1967, Section 2, pp. 1, 11. Culkin asserts that the average student has watched television for 15,000 hours by the time he graduates from high school. He concludes: "Their psychological intake system is programmed for the moving image."

[2] Stanley Kauffmann, *A World on Film* (New York, 1966), pp. 415-428.

On the Theory of Film as History 49

by the professional historian devoted to an essentially humanistic and "liberal" quest for the constantly evolving definition of man in time.[3]

Because film is not only an art form, but at the same time an industry and one of the mass entertainment and communications media, its value to the social historian is further increased. The role which the cinema plays in contemporary entertainment for the world's population is phenomenal. In 1964, about 4,000 feature films are officially known to have been produced in the world.[4] Over 19,000,000,000 movie tickets were sold during the same year,[5] which means the same as if every human being in the world had attended the movies an average of nearly six times a year! If it were possible to add to these figures accurate statistics regarding the number of people who saw films on television the results would be even more staggering.

"Film is one of the most expensive of the media of communication."[6] With the rarest of exceptions feature films require enormous investments and are made with the idea of gaining a financial return in the entertainment market.[7] Much of the socio-historical analysis of art in recent years has centered on the

---

[3] R. F. Arragon, "Encounter with the Humanities," *The Key Reporter,* XXXII (Summer, 1967), 2-4.

[4] *United Nations Statistical Yearbook 1967* (New York, 1967), pp. 756-757. This is an approximation since the basis for counting varies in the different countries. There were no figures for some important producers, such as the Soviet Union and the Philippines, so production figures for the next closest year reported were included, adding another 500 films to the total.

[5] *Ibid.,* pp. 760-761. This is also an approximation since the total is based upon figures for the most recent available years. The French film historian, Philippe Esnault, in a lecture at the *Institut des Hautes Études Cinématographiques* in Paris on October 6, 1967, asserted that more people see films now in one year than have attended the theater in all its history.

[6] Raymond Spottiswoode, *Film and its Techniques* (Berkeley and Los Angeles, 1965), p. 6.

[7] A profound change is under way today as film equipment becomes cheaper and thus more available to the young; as one of the dominant film styles rejects technical

question of patronage, where the patron has been seen to be a vital link between a work of art and society and an inescapable factor to be considered when evaluating the social reflectivity of art. For the cinema the ultimate patrons are the masses of people who pay their way into the movie theaters. It is thus inevitable that since the film industry is dependent upon mass support for the financial solvency essential for mere continuation, it would be more than usually sensitive to mass interests and mass desires.

"Every film is a document concerning the people who have made it and the people who have seen it."[8] The cinema is a recorder and preserver of its time, a mine of captured visual detail. It is also a reflector of the elusive and the unstated, of social mores, attitudes and values, and of the psycho-social realities of specific societies at given periods in time, and at least since arriving at its first plateau in its evolution as an art form – the classical period of the silent cinema in the 1920's – it has been as well a force in history, a mover of men, an active agent in the evolution of human society.

Because there is, as Arnold Hauser has asserted, a "fundamental naturalism" connected with the film, because the film "is the only art that takes over considerable pieces of reality unaltered,"[9] and because one of the most obvious uses to which a film can be put is the simple recording of visual reality, the captured visual detail is almost always present. Such detail can be part of an imaginative

---

perfection; as distribution circuits become less a monopoly of the major studios. Films are being made for far less money. A significant historical exception to the rule that films are made to earn money was the practice of the Vicomte de Noailles of producing a film for his wife on her birthday. This permitted the creation of such important works as Man Ray's *Le Mystère du Chateau de Dès,* Cocteau's *Blood of a Poet,* and Bunuel's *L'Age d'Or.* See *Etudes Cinematographiques,* nos. 38-39, 40-42, 1965, 2 vols., I, 22-23.

[8] Esnault, lecture, October 6, 1967.

[9] Arnold Hauser, *The Philosophy of Art History* (New York, 1959), p. 363. Or as Raymond Spottiswoode has expressed it in *Film and its Technique,* p. 19, the camera as an instrument of artistic creation uses "the stuff of the outside world, the world of green things, of land and sea, of human beings and the places where they work and live." The raw material of the film is whatever of concrete, physical reality cinematographically recorded.

reconstruction, and although less valuable as source material, can still be meaningfully used in teaching. Bergman's *The Seventh Seal* is a good example. Many of the visual elements of this beautiful film were inspired by some late medieval frescoes illustrating the spirit of the waning Middle Ages which had terrified Bergman as a boy.[10]

Of greater historical importance, because of its value as source material, is the captured visual detail when the film deals with a period contemporary with its creation. This is true even when such a record is totally unintended. The early films of Louis Lumière, the French pioneer of the film industry, such as *The Arrival of the Train in the Station* and *The Card Party*, intended nothing other than the exploitation of the novelty of seeing motion reproduced and yet they have recorded and preserved the costumes and attitudes of a French provincial bourgeoisie at the end of the nineteenth century. The Humphrey Bogart crime films of the 1940's have recorded in much the same way various aspects of American urban life of the period, such as architecture, traffic patterns, car design, and fashions. These films have thus already become an important source of significant visual detail for future urban historians.

Perhaps of greatest historical importance as a visual record are newsreels and documentaries contemporary with the events they describe. Less than two months after the first public demonstration in Paris of Lumière's movie projector, representatives of the firm, trained to operate both a camera and a projector, were sent from France to demonstrate the equipment in other countries. Demonstration was only part of their mission. They also made films of daily life or important events, in whatever country they were, sending these films back to France to be shown there.[11] They had been given instructions to "Open your lenses upon the world," and film criticism in 1895 already described the work of Lumière's cameramen as "nature taken alive" or "nature caught in

---

[10] Jacques Sicher, *Ingmar Bergman* (Paris, 1960), pp. 118-119.

[11] Pierre Leprohom, *Histoire du Cinéma,* 2 vols. (Paris, 1961), I, 25, 35.

the act."[1,2] Newsreels — cinematic newspapers — have existed as a genre of film production since the early years of the twentieth century. All the belligerent nations sent film crews to the various fronts during the First World War.[13] In the inter-war period, even in the democracies, governmental departments subsidized the visual recording of those aspects of their society's existence coming under their competence.[14] Much of the material has been lost, but enormous quantities remain.

During the past decade a spate of feature-length films have appeared, edited from archival materials which have survived. Paris in 1900, World War I, the Russian Revolution, the Spanish Civil War, Nazi Germany, the Nuremberg trials — to name only a few — have all been the subject of such edited historical documentaries. The persuasiveness of film creates both an opportunity that historians must not permit to pass unexploited and a responsibility which they must not fail to assume. Most of these films cited are either flagrant examples of bias or examples equally flagrant of insipid commentary exploiting the temporally exotic.

The film can be an invaluable aid to historical teaching and an irreplaceable historical source as a visual record. Leni Riefenstahl's *The Triumph of the Will*, commissioned and paid for by the Nazis, using the spectacularly staged party rallies in Nuremberg as material for an undisguised propaganda film, has become today a dramatic instrument for demonstrating to the contemporary student, far removed from the attitudes, hopes, and fears of the 1930's, the appeal of fascism. In various American film archives[15] there are materials for thousands of studies on specific subjects: the evolution of cities, changing fashions of dress and what they

---

[12] Spottiswoode, *Film and its Technique*, p. 21, n. 1.

[13] Philippe Esnault, "Toute la Mémoire du Monde," *Image et Son*, No. 188, November, 1965, pp. 42-43.

[14] In Great Britain under first the Empire Marketing Board and then the General Post Office, a film unit under the direction of John Grierson has provided historians with a remarkable record of some aspects of British life during the period. Less was done in the United States, but Flaherty's *The Land*, produced for the Department of Agriculture (and not released at the time because of its compelling picture of rural misery) is an example of what does exist.

[15] To which must now be added the vast archives of television.

reveal about social attitudes, views on race and such problems, or examinations of relatively distinct historical periods such as the New Deal. All these things can and should be analyzed as historical source material, then composed and expressed visually for use in the teaching of history.

The cinema has been inadequately investigated by the historian thus far in terms of its being a recorder and preserver of significant visual detail. Even less adequately has it been investigated as a reflector of changing social attitudes and values, the intangibles which are the cement of a society or are the motive force leading to changes in its structures. The human experience given form in any art work changes with time and geography as well as with societal structures and metaphysical presuppositions. American optimism is reflected (and perhaps fed?) by the traditional Hollywood "happy ending." Films made twenty years ago already shock the changed social sensitivities of contemporary audiences. In *Red Dust,* a typical commercial vehicle for Clark Gable and Jean Harlow, while the amorous duel between the two runs its preordained course, Gable evidences in a few characterization scenes a racism and an American acceptance of colonial exploitation that many contemporary filmgoers would find appalling.[16] Yet such behavior went largely unnoticed at the time. It was accepted as normal and natural by the masses who frequented the theaters.

The historical analysis of film as a reflector of society can be approached in two ways. The first is to consider the film as the work of one man, usually the director, but sometimes the screenwriter. This is the "author approach" so dear to modern European critics. Here the total production of one man, Marcel L'Herbier or Sergei Eisenstein or Michelangelo Antonioni, is subjected to examination to reveal recurrent themes, significant formal styles, and elements of film language revelatory of one man's relationship to the society and epoch in which he lives or lived. This is done in much the same way as the analysis of the works of Proust or Joyce or Hemingway and with similar

---

[16] Peter Noble has studied the pervasive racism in films in *The Negro in Films,* London, 1948.

objectives, potential results, and limitations. In both cases the assumption is made that the creators possess a sensitivity peculiar to artists that permits them to feel and to describe — if not necessarily to understand — things about their societies of which the average member is either totally unaware or only most nebulously conscious.

The second approach is much closer to sociology and concerns itself less with film as the artistic creation of one man than with the total film production of one society at one given period of time. It is much more concerned with French films of the 1920's than with Marcel L'Herbier, more with Soviet pre-war film production than with Eisenstein, more with Italian neo-realism than with Antonioni. As an approach this resembles the examination of *all* novels of a society at a certain moment in time (or, for manageability, of a random sample), not just those which having passed through the critical sieve of history are considered great. Here what is looked for are trends, shifts in attitudes, similarities in the questions posed or reactions recorded that seem to run through a variety of different artistic expressions. When individual differences of personality and sensitivities are deliberately eliminated, does there remain a certain body of common concerns, common attitudes, common values? What is there common to the work of Eisenstein, Pudovkin and Dovzhenko? What does this tell us about Soviet society? What sort of heroes are proposed to society in these films? What are their attitudes, values and goals?[17] What specific conflicts have been selected to give dramatic motion to the story? What themes are treated by preference? It is a well-known phenomenon of movie production that a film innovative in theme or treatment which becomes a huge commercial success (hence reflecting the desires or at least remaining within the boundaries of attitudes acceptable to a mass audience) immediately engenders a whole series of films varying

---

[17] A fascinating study could be made of film stars and the images they created and sustained that would reveal much about the evolution of a society's attitudes and values. There is a world of difference between the images of Lillian Gish and Marilyn Monroe or those of Douglas Fairbanks and Marlon Brando. Cf. the treatment given this subject by Edgar Morin in *Les Stars* (Paris, 1957), and Pierre Leprohon, *Le Monde du Cinéma*, (Paris, 1967).

only slightly in theme or treatment from the successful "pilot" or "model" film.[18] Have significant changes appeared in "remakes" which parallel attitudes of contemporary production?

Although films would naturally provide the core of materials analyzed in such an approach, they cannot be meaningfully studied in isolation. The investigator must have more than a passing acquaintance with the major historical events and concerns of the society or the period. He must be familiar with tendencies as expressed in the other coincident art forms. He would have to draw upon contemporaneous critical reaction to the film in question to have a clearer conception of what it meant to audiences of the time.

These suggested approaches to film as a reflector of society can best be illustrated briefly by a glance first at the work of two recognized post-war "authors," Ingmar Bergman and Michelangelo Antonioni, and even at the differences and similarities which existed in the film production of Germany, France and the Soviet Union between the two world wars.

It would be a profound mistake to treat the works of the two men — or of any filmmaker — as one would those of Wittgenstein or Sartre. The director's is rarely, if ever, a seminal mind. His importance lies elsewhere — in popularization, in vulgarization of contemporary intellectual currents, or in bringing to essentially mass audiences a heightened awareness of a contemporary situation and its implications. <u>The psychological impact of the cinema, its inherent powers of persuasion, make it an irreplaceable link between intellectual speculation and mass consciousness.</u>

Future intellectual historians concerned with the religious or metaphysical questions of western society in the decades following World War II will have to include the films of Ingmar Bergman in their analyses and judgments. Bergman's continuing concerns include the cinematic exploration of twentieth century man's relationship to God and the problems of human communication and solitude as viewed in a metaphysical context. Neither the content of his films nor the composition of his typical audiences

---

[18] *Easy Rider* and *Bob and Carol and Ted and Alice* have already produced many descendants.

would suggest that his are, truly speaking, mass films. Rather, they reflect the concerns of, and hence appeal to, a relatively large and well-educated international public. They are not the reflection of the mass "return to religion" movement of wartime and the immediate post-war period, nor do they bear witness to the growing separation between religion and daily life expressed in mounting religious indifference. They echo the anguished outcry of men nurtured in a culture whose roots are, in large part, Christian and to whom these roots appear withered if not already dead. The outcry is an anguished one because these men are not indifferent to the loss. They wish to believe in a divine presence in the universe but can no longer accept the traditional concepts which translated this faith in a meaningful manner. Historical skepticism and daily contact with the essentially positivist and materialist values of contemporary society have thoroughly eroded the possibility of such acceptance.

From the *Seventh Seal* through the "trilogy" (*Through a Glass Darkly, Winter Light,* and *The Silence*) to *Persona,* Bergman has returned again and again to a treatment of these themes and their implications. The resolution he suggests is in perfect harmony with the contemporary institutional evolution of Christianity — Protestant and Catholic alike — as well as with what has been called the New Humanism of the post-World War II epoch. Meaning and significance must be sought first and foremost in man (not Man but the individual), in the human, in life, no matter how frightening or horrible man or life can be.[19] What is important to man, what is most real, what is most understandable is his own human experience. He can go beyond this to the universal, but he must begin here.

Antonioni's major films may be said to begin at the point reached by Bergman in *Persona*: the transcendental is totally absent; the utterly human is the focal point of attention. Like Godard, Antonioni in his trilogy (*L'Avventura, La Notte* and *L'Eclisse*), in *Red Desert, Blow-Up* and *Zabriskie Point,* functions as a cinematic journalist of our times. But unlike Godard, he is

---

[19] *Hour of the Wolf* and *Shame* push to extreme limits Bergman's vision of human potential for degradation and the horrible.

almost uniquely concerned with states of mind and attitudes, not actions and socio-political options. Antonioni's world is primarily urban, coldly functional, bourgeois, and materially comfortable. His characters are solitary, locked in themselves through an inability to communicate, and terribly conscious of their incapacity to love because of this inability. Or, because of a profound confusion regarding their essential selves, they are condemned by the temporal fragility of love, or forced to pursue its momentary substitute, the transitory satisfaction of purely physical sex. They are disengaged people because engagement is commitment and commitment derives from self-knowledge and ability to love to the point of acting. Antonioni is not attempting a Human Comedy of our epoch, but he is making a significant record of a certain segment of contemporary western society which is bored because its material goals have been reached to surfeit, confused because it remains ignorant of itself, despairing because of the dissolution of traditional values and the eclipse of meaning.

Neither Bergman nor Antonioni will ever tell future historians all there is to know about our epoch, but nor will any one philosopher or novelist. Their concern with certain dominant themes, however, and the public response to their concern will provide an important source for future social analysts as well as a visual record of our life captured and preserved by them on film.

To turn from the "author" approach to the more sociological one, the inter-war period can provide an excellent illustration, since the period is one of confusion, vacillation, and political hesitation between the past and the future. It is a period where at one and the same time old structures and attitudes were questioned and immense efforts were expended to preserve or resuscitate them *in toto*. It is one in which for almost every industrially advanced society a "Decade of Illusion" was spent vainly seeking to recover the "Lost Paradise" of pre-war Europe. This was almost universally followed by the brutal awakening brought about by the Great Depression which ushered in a painful decade forcefully revealing a whole new series of political, economic, and social realities. It is a period, then, in which the sub-conscious, the intangible, the sub-surface ground-swell can with proper treatment be more revelatory of significant changes in the values, attitudes, desires, and objectives of these societies than the conscious and publicly articulated aims and programs.

The contemporaneous internal evolution of film production further heightens the possibility of attaining fruitful results. The inter-war period witnessed the appearance of *national* production, films increasingly influenced by the conditions under which they were produced and distributed, the degree of censorship or governmental interest, and the attitudes and desires of the masses whose support was necessary for the continuation of production.[20]

Three national "schools" made explosive entries into the film world during this period: German expressionism, the French avant-garde (impressionism and surrealism), and Soviet documentary realism. No one of these schools ever completely dominated the total film production in their respective countries. But significant insight can be gained and certain questions raised by an analysis of these particular schools. When viewed in conjunction with tendencies expressed in the other arts, as well as the socio-political evolutions of their respective societies, they all reflect an awareness of the crumbling of the old order and a search for new certainties.

These three schools taken together are fascinating for just this reason. On the surface they have nothing in common. German expressionism was quite theatrical in nature and employed the arts of painting and architecture and the modeling power of light creatively as integral parts of the cinematic experience. The French avant-garde was much more purely technically oriented. It sought to break noisily with everything which was theatrical, everything which was literature, everything which could be expressed through another medium.[21] The result was an incredibly effervescent experimentation with the possibilities of the camera — mobility, distortion, superimposition, angle, and focus. Soviet documentary realism, as its name implies, insisted upon the

---

[20] This does not mean that films displayed *no* national characteristics prior to this period, but this is the first time that one can speak of an actual national film production.

[21] Henri Fescourt, *La Foi et les Montagnes* (Paris, 1959), pp. 227-228.

nature of the movie camera as an observer, a recorder of reality. Even in their theories of montage, where the Soviet theorists departed most completely from the view of film making as passive recording, they insisted upon the visual elements, the individual shots, being natural, common, and everyday in character. They insisted further that the themes treated should be similar in nature and that the style of montage, i.e., putting the shots into the desired sequence at the desired rhythm, employ a dialectical relationship of visual images from which would arise another, distinct but related, and greater reality.

The three schools seem to be so different and yet they can be understood as merely three different expressions of the revolutionary impact of World War I already vaguely sensed by the artists and beginning to be analyzed by the intellectuals. These modes of expression differed in part because of the differing internal evolution of movie-making in the three countries,[22] in part because of different artistic traditions in the other arts,[23] in part because of the manner in which film-making was organized in the three countries.[24]

---

[22] In France, although the first films are credited to Lumière, a film by Meliès appeared almost at the same time. Meliès was a man who was fascinated by and immediately began exploring the possibilities of illusion inherent in the processes of film making. The generation of French film makers of the 1920's, reacting against the work of the previous generation, denounced the "art film" which was theatrical in nature, personnel, and subject matter and vigorously proclaimed the supremacy of the visual in the cinema. In Germany which also experienced the beginning of film making in the Lumière-like slice-of-life documentaries of Skladanovsky, the theatre very quickly began playing a formative role. In the inter-war period, an often underestimated strain of German film production, the so-called "realistic" strain, was inspired by (and seldom went further than) the somewhat romanticized concern with social reality of Max Reinhardt's *Kammerspiel*. In Russia, the October Revolution marks a caesura in film production with many of the older generation of directors, technicians, and actors emigrating. This brought to the fore the younger generation of film makers who had been cinematically born and raised on wartime documentaries.

[23] Briefly stated, in painting expressionism was native to Germany, impressionism to France, while surrealist headquarters for all the arts was Paris. Socialist realism, which was later to weigh so heavily on Soviet art, has much in common with Soviet film production. They both share a didactic concern with social realities and the compositional elements of both are taken from the common and easily recognizable daily experience of those at whom the works were aimed.

[24] In Germany expressionist films were the result of a conscious decision on the part of UFA, the film monopoly whose roots went back to the Hindenburg-Ludendorff "total

The nature and character of film production of these three schools, apparently so different, when seen from a certain perspective reveal a basically similar reaction to the aftermath of the war. The old order had ended. The certainties of the nineteenth century European bourgeois civilization had to be questioned if not denied outright. The "realities" of this civilization — whether intellectual, social, metaphysical, or formal ceased to be important; they had been drained of all vitality in the bloodletting of 1914-1918. For the German expressionists, what *had* been considered real was only the surface. The more real lay in the subjective realm of the mental and the instinctual, in dream and imagination and myth, in subconsciously existing desires and fears. The real reality, the only certainty, was internal and had to be externalized, had to be *expressed*.[25]

For the French surrealists, the search was similar and had similar roots. The nineteenth century "real" was an illusion. The fundamental was the *sur*real, that which was above and beyond the traditional real. And this new reality demanded new structures, new forms, new relationships for its expression. We are accustomed to view surrealism as purely an artistic movement, but

---

mobilization." The decision was made in an attempt to find a product sufficiently different to compete nationally and internationally with a disastrously competitive Hollywood. In France no such single monopoly existed, and in the almost anarchic situation of French film production, ample opportunity was provided and impulse given to the technical experimentation of any director who found the money to make a film. In Soviet Russia, Lenin immediately recognized the propaganda potential of the film. Soviet film production was nationalized and put to the service of the revolution. The similarity between Marxist metaphysics and Soviet film theory is striking. These parallels in theory were further reinforced by the material conditions of production. Shut off from the West, and thereby from the raw film producing Occident, Soviet Russia experienced an excruciating shortage of raw film stock. What had to be told, had to be told quickly and with the employment of as little film as possible. The use of exposed film preserved in the archives, frequently documentary footage, offered an opportunity for further savings of invaluable raw film. And if the propaganda purposes of film making were to be satisfied, the "message" had to be clear, easily accessible to the largely uneducated masses, and thus expressed in visual terms having experiential resonance in their own lives.

[25] Rudolf Kurtz, *Expressionismus und Film* (Berlin, 1926, photographically reproduced by Verlag Hans Rohr, Zurich, 1965), p. 14.

On the Theory of Film as History

to the surrealists themselves this was only part of their existence. Art was to them only an instrument, an instrument of the total revolution they were preparing which aimed at the full liberation of man.[26] As it was nineteenth century bourgeois civilization and certitude which were under attack, bourgeois convictions had to be shaken. Nothing was spared to "shock the bourgeoisie." On the screen an eyeball was slit with a razor, an ecclesiastical dignitary appeared as a skeleton clothed in the rich vestments of the church, human beings floated through the air, while a funeral procession became a hilarious exercise in incongruity. The romantic love and feminine domesticity so prized by the middle classes gave way to paeans of praise for sensuality and sexual passion.[27] The old order was crumbling. It would have to be destroyed.

This concern with a new order of reality was no less present in Soviet documentary realism, although there it was more specifically limited to social reality. The old order was cinematically expressed in part to explain how and why the revolution took place, and in part to emphasize by contrast the progress made since the revolution. But the accent was emphatically placed upon the emergent new order, the development of new social relationships liberating man from the exploitation of the old ways. Whether in France, Germany, or Soviet Russia, a significant number of films of the epoch, despite differences in approach, all reflected a growing consciousness of the decline of the civilization inherited from the nineteenth century and a desire for its destruction, a consciousness and a desire running counter to the frantic efforts of many politicians and statesmen to resuscitate the old order.

---

[26] Here again is a parallel between the three schools – the goal of liberation. For expressionism, externalizing the more basic drives of man, was to be a means of liberating him from the artificial bonds of bourgeois inhibitions, and Soviet documentary realism was seen as an instrument in the propagation of the revolution, itself the historically necessary instrument in the liberation of the masses from class exploitation. See *Études Cinématographiques*, I, 24-25, 57-58, 98-99, 105; II, 153, 160, 181, 199-200.

[27] This, too, aimed at the revolutionary liberation of man. See Robert Desnos, *Cinéma*, ed. by Andre Tchernia (Paris, 1966), pp. 101-103, 153-155, 159-160.

Film, then, can be analyzed by the historian as a recorder and preserver of significant visual detail and as a reflector of social mores, attitudes, and values. Films offer still another and related area for scholarly study because like newspapers, they not only report and reflect, but are in themselves a force for change or stability. Films are not only a source of history; they are one of the motors of history, and because of their psychological impact, a very influential one. This impact derives primarily from four factors: the nature of the film experience, the control exercised by the filmmaker over that which the spectator sees, the inherent concreteness of the visual image, and the conditions under which a film is viewed.

The film experience is not, as is commonly held, a passive experience. It is in its very essence one of participation by the spectator. Film was created as a means of fulfilling a centuries-old desire of man, to reproduce motion. But film actually creates only the *illusion* of motion as well as that of three-dimensionality on a plane surface. It does this through manipulating light and capitalizing upon that peculiarity of the human eye, the retina which retains an image 1/10 of a second after that image's light source has already disappeared. In the projection of a film, light is passed through a celluloid band of varying transparency which itself moves with regular but discontinuous motion between a source of light and a lens. When projected upon a reflecting screen, this light produces plane surfaces of varying brightness or different colors. That which is perceived as motion on the screen is nothing but a series of disjunctive plane surfaces which "persistence of vision" composes into unified motion. Film is founded upon an illusion and the illusion is achieved only through the spectator's unwilled and unconscious participation. Most cinematic effects depend upon the spectator entering the theater with a whole series of visual reactions formed by his daily experience.

Rooted in the spectator's participation, the film experience has undergone an evolution which has increased that participation. The first conscious development of film in this direction was the work of the Brighton School in Britain and Edwin S. Porter in the early years of the twentieth century when they decomposed the continuous scene into its component shots and the spectator was asked to create the temporal and spatial continuity himself. Then Griffith in alternate montage (e.g., preparations for an execution alternating with a feverish race to stop it) asked the spectator to achieve the psychological unity of two spatially separated but temporally parallel events. The next step was taken when the Soviet school of documentary realism systematically extended Griffith's practices of alternate montage to symbolic parallels. The conceptual unity was to be created and emotionally enlarged by the spectator himself through his identification of two factually quite distinct events possessing parallel implications (e.g., shots of strikers being mown down by soldiers alternating with shots of a slaughter-house).

In the late 1920's, as silent cinematography reached a peak of expressiveness, film makers turned increasingly to the symbolic image to expand the dimensions of more prosaic sequences. This, of course, made greater demands upon the spectator for active intellectual and emotional participation in the final creation of meaning and significance and, incidentally, increasingly presumed a capacity of the audience for such participation. After the interlude of the 1930's and 1940's, when a fascination with sound condemned the spectator to a theatrical and explicit verbalism, Italian neo-realism again promoted increased spectator participation, but now less in terms of technique than in those of thematic significance and social realism.[28]

The control of the film maker over what the spectator sees and the length of time he sees it enormously increases the director's power to persuade. The variable distance between the spectator and the drama taking place on the screen imparts to the film a whole range of expression which derives from symbolic use of detail. In a film, if the director decides that the audience should notice a nervous wringing of the hands, the close-up eliminates all other possibilities of distracting the viewer from this one detail. The spectator might not see *all* that the director wishes him to see, but he can never see *more* than the director wishes him to see.

---

[28] Federico Fellini in a radio interview with Gideon Bachmann transcribed for *Film Book I*, edited by Robert Hughes (New York, 1959), pp. 97-105, and reprinted in Richard Dyer MacCann, *Film, A Montage of Theories* (New York, 1966), p. 381.

As compared with literature and poetry the film differentiates itself in the precise manner by which the visual image differentiates itself from the word – by a precision and a concreteness that the latter does not possess. Film is inescapably concrete even when concerned with the inhabitants of our dream worlds or imaginations. The unicorn, the ghost, and the vampire possess on the screen the same degree of reality and concreteness as the stone, the battleship, and the dog. Film affects us because of the *illusion* it creates of reality. As all is illusion, all is equally real.²⁹

The conditions under which a film is viewed further intensifies the power of film to persuade and to influence. In a movie theater, the only source of light, sound, and motion is the screen. This means that the spectator's attention is automatically and almost forcibly concentrated upon what the screen is conveying. The eye may wander, but very little; it is almost impossible to ignore motion or light. When this is coupled with a dramatic problem, one's psychological attention is equally engaged. Although as has been seen, the film experience is far from a passive one, it is during the time that it is occurring, usually an uncritical one. The spectator lives in an eternal present of sensory stimulation where he has neither the time nor the possibility to stop the experience in order to reflect a bit or to go back. Each moment brings a great amount of information which the spectator can only register at the time; he cannot weigh, select, and discard.

The impact of films can be readily observed, if only superficially, in such things as hair and clothing styles – Brigitte Bardot hairdos and *Bonnie and Clyde* outfits. Is it too much to expect that movies could do the same thing for attitudes and values? Lenin did not think so and acted rapidly to set up a film institute

---

²⁹The tricks of the cinema are legion and well-known, but when well done, are always convincing. In 1940 Len Lye produced an anti-fascist film, *Hitler Parade,* in which Hitler appeared doing a ridiculous dance to a popular English tune. The sequence was tricked by interrupting forward motion, reversing it, and accelerating it rhythmically. A film strip in which Hitler was perhaps only walking was transformed into a propaganda film in which he was made ludicrous as a dancer. This film is still cited in serious works on Hitler and is still included in montage films on the Nazis as "Hitler dancing with joy at the news of the French defeat." The concreteness of the visual image persuades the spectator of its reality, and hence its truth." Georges Sadoul, *Les Merveilles du Cinéma* (Paris, 1957), p. 143.

as well as a film control board to produce and to supervise ideologically films which were to play an active role in explaining and winning support for the Soviet revolution.[30] Goebbels in Nazi Germany did much the same. The continuing controversy surrounding censorship not only in totalitarian countries, but in the so-called Free World further testifies to a belief in and a fear of the influence of films.[31] Young film makers, especially in Europe and the developing countries, are now speaking of a "cinema of revolution."[32] Godard, with each successive film, is making it clearer that he hopes to prepare the way for profound societal change by shocking and disgusting people, by making them mock at and be repelled by what he feels is the absurdity of contemporary society.

This is obviously a potentially very pregnant area for sociological or socio-psychological analysis. What, for example, is the role of the "Western" in preserving the myth of rugged individualism in American values in an epoch when it is considered by many people no longer valid? What indeed is the role of the Western in *creating* the myth since obviously cooperation and community togetherness played at least as great a role in the conquest of the West as did the lonely actions of self-reliant and decisive men? What is the connection between the Hollywood happy ending and a fundamental American optimism? Even if, as can be presumed, the optimism preceded the inevitability of the happy ending, what has the latter done to preserve or encourage the continuation of this optimism? There is much talk of a contemporary revolution in morals. What role have films played in encouraging this revolution? These and many similar questions deserve the attention of the humanists and the social scientists interested in the workings of our society. A sociology of film impact carried out on contemporary audiences of contemporary films could become an

---

[30] Georges Sadoul in *Histoire du Cinéma Mondial* (Paris, 1961), p. 172 cites the phrase of Lenin in 1922, soon "taken as an order": "Of all the arts, cinema is the most important to us."

[31] See Richard Dyer MacCann, *Film and Society* (New York, 1964), pp. 89-128.

[32] *Le Monde*, January, 1968.

invaluable theoretical tool for the historian to apply to what is already the historical past.[33]

Even now the historian could apply the existing tools of his discipline to such projects as the analysis of propaganda films. These are films consciously made to promote certain goals, to persuade, to unite, and to stimulate to action. It is this consciousness, this purposiveness, which gives to the propaganda film its distinct value for socio-psychological analysis. The historian should bring to the study of such films a series of questions: What goals are being proposed? What aspects of human life are being emphasized? What values are being appealed to in order to promote the ends desired? What social attitudes are presupposed to be normal? What is the nature of the menace considered to be threatening the society either from within or from without? Responses to these questions when found to be generalized in the propaganda films regardless of the specific subject treated would provide invaluable insights into the human and social psychology of the society studied. In the propaganda film, the attitudes and values of a society, normally the backdrop for dramatic action, come into the foreground and stand naked for analysis.

The potential of professional historical attention to films is indeed vast in terms both of teaching and research. Whether used as illustration or source, whether regarded as recorder, reflector, or motor, film merits much more serious study than has been the practice in the United States. Ours is an increasingly visual age and one in which a revolution in communications is transforming our society. The generation of students now on college campuses, whatever their disciplines might be, know films, take them seriously, are open to and stimulated by what films have to say. The near absence of scholarly attention to the past and present of cinematic production is a negligence which educators and humanist scholars can ill afford.

---

[33] See Mortimer Adler, "Research: The Immature" on the Payne Fund research projects, in MacCann, *Film and Society,* pp. 85-86.

Film and Style: The Fictional Documentary

JOAN MELLEN

The mid-nineteen sixties saw in world cinema a renaissance of the fictional documentary, films rooted in concrete historical contexts whose action expressed the social conflicts of the decade and in some cases the century. In literature this form was developed during the same period by the "nonfictional novel," exemplified in Norman Mailer's *The Armies of the Night*. Both nonfiction novel and fictional documentary aspire to revitalize their art in implicit protest against the retreat from commitment to a moral asceticism epitomized by Susan Sontag's influential essay, "Against Interpretation."

Many of the new filmmakers who emerged during the sixties wished to rediscover social conflict and to renew the political film. Critics of the fifties, still reacting to the communist art of the twenties and thirties, argued that art possessed of social or political conviction must be either propaganda or crudely didactic, echoing Hemingway's facile quip, "If you've got a message, send a telegram." In part this response was a consequence of the general disillusionment with the crassness and dishonest sentimentality of Soviet art under Stalin. These new filmmakers rescued political art from such grotesque didacticism, and reestablished moral concerns and social consciousness in art by bringing to such values the nuance and psychological range essential to any work of merit no matter its nominal subject.

Prominent among them were several Italian directors: Bernardo Bertolucci, Gillo Pontecorvo, Elio Petri and Giuliano Montaldo. They include Costa-Gavras, a Greek exile working in France, the Swedish filmmaker Bo Widerberg and the Swiss Jean-Luc Godard, whose oeuvre itself has undergone a transformation from new wave experimentation to radical political critique. Their art is in

---

*Copyright © 1973 by The Antioch Review, Inc. First published in *The Antioch Review*, Vol. 32, No. 3, pp. 403-425; reprinted by permission of the editor; also reprinted in Joan Mellen, *Taking Aim: Films about Politics*.

defiance of Sontag's tenet that "to interpret is to impoverish, to deplete the world — in order to set up a shadow world of 'meanings' " as opposed to its possible "pure, untranslatable, sensuous immediacy."[1] These directors, to the contrary, explore the history of the recent past. Their work argues that it is precisely a history without "meaning" which impoverishes. For them it is the tacit assent to mystification of the political which "depletes" our world.

Many of these artists are of the left. Godard declares himself a militant Maoist. Others of them have been identified with the official Communist movement. Pontecorvo remains close to the Communist Party in Italy, although he left it formally in 1956. Elio Petri, a Marxist, has said, "without the Communist Party, we would live here [in Italy] as in Spain under Franco."[2] Bertolucci remains a member of the Italian Communist Party. Costa-Gavras' energetic criticism of existing parties and state powers admits to no ready ideological designation beyond his Marxism. The films of these men are successful when the director is personally engaged and feels a powerful identification with his protagonists or with the circumstances he chooses to depict. Such films have become art when their directors have created both for themselves and for the audience an enlarged awareness of why and how war, social injustice, class exploitation and imperialism continue to plague us.

Where the director is ambivalent or unwilling to commit himself to a particular point of view about the historical circumstances which provide the subject of his film, the fictional documentary mode proves inappropriate. The film, like Losey's *Assassination of Trotsky* (1972) or Costa-Gavras' *The Confession* (1970), becomes evasive and even dishonest. Commitment by itself, of course, in no way assures a realized film; but only deep involvement in the events allows a filmmaker to produce a many-sided view of political and social stress. Pontecorvo's *The Battle of Algiers* (1966) is a clear example. A critical self-consciousness given to constant testing of ideas and actions strongly espoused is as important to the life of the historical documentary as is the choice

---

[1] Susan Sontag, *Against Interpretation* (New York, 1966), pp. 7, 9.

[2] From personal conversations in Rome, May, 1972.

of subject matter. If Godard and Costa-Gavras are less accomplished than Pontecorvo and Bertolucci, it is because their passion misleads them to reduce the struggle they depict, unwittingly diminishing their values and protagonists by the concealment of complex motive and uneven consciousness.

There is a clear connection between the student and worker radical politics of the 1960s in France and Italy and the emergence of these filmmakers at the height of their powers. The general strike and near insurrection in France (1968) and Italy (1969) disproved the analysts, ranging from liberals to Herbert Marcuse, who portrayed the workers as assimilated, bought off or reactionary. The possibility of social and political change in the advanced industrial countries seemed feasible for the first time since the end of the Second World War. The death of Stalin had earlier liberated many intellectuals from the appalling inclination to identify radical change with a police regime. Once Khrushchev acknowledged, if only partially, the dissociation between Stalin and revolutionary practice, these intellectuals of the Left no longer had to apologize for the conservatism and the crimes of the Soviet Union. They were free at last to explore real models for socialism.

In Italy, France and Japan, young filmmakers were stirred by the social ferment surrounding them. Militantly political filmmakers like Godard and Marco Bellocchio were encouraged in the notion that cinema could perform a major cultural role in the transvaluation of values preliminary to mass radicalization. Young artists like Bertolucci, whose concerns were as much with aesthetic as political problems, found in historical subjects a means of expressing both.

The work of these filmmakers cannot be assessed solely by aesthetic criteria. Because each of their films, in its own way, presents us with a revision of our own history, they must also be considered for the clarity with which they illuminate real events. Artistic and intellectual rigor are inextricably dependent upon an ability to synthesize feelings of inadequacy, confusion and discontent – our sense of being trapped in alien social systems within which we must define our lives. These directors believe that their own work and the medium itself are enriched by the historical density of their subjects. What makes them particularly interesting is that none of them shrinks from attempting rational explanation and even remedy merely because cultural orthodoxy has decreed that convictions or solutions diminish the felt life of a film.

From Nouvelle Vague to Fictional Documentary

Implicit in the view of human relations which treats them exclusively within the realm of personal experience, is the assumption of a stable social milieu in which larger conflicts have been essentially resolved.[3] The culture which accompanies a period of apparent stasis turns to formal questions of style for their own sake and to a psychology of character which views human beings as distant if not isolated from the broad social and intellectual influences which have given them shape.

When human activity is assumed to be unrelated to and incapable of changing social values and institutions, the preoccupation of orthodox art is with its own conventions and the decorum of manner. Its psychology, because it is immutable, often becomes cynical (as in the case of the early Godard) or despairing (as evidenced by the films of Michelangelo Antonioni). Roots of disintegration within people are unrelated to alienation from belief in the possibility of human improvement, liberation or change. The suppression of strong feeling, the presence of anxiety and the experience of ambivalence in individuals are then regarded apart from society and from the mores which imprint upon the personal psyche a particular social form.

Such periods are accompanied by tendencies toward decadence in art. This mood was given theoretical formulation in the novels and films of both Alain Robbe-Grillet in France and Susan Sontag in the United States. In the case of both, their novels and films early exhausted themselves. In film, with the exception of the limited and shrill psychological dramas of filmed theatre produced with regularity by Ingmar Bergman, the noncommitted art of the late fifties and early sixties has almost completely disappeared.

---

[3]This was the dominant sensibility enshired by the French *nouvelle vague*, including, during the early sixties, such directors as Claude Chabrol, Francois Truffaut and Godard.

The form itself of the drama of ennui was too narrow to contain the genre of film. At its greatest moments, in Russia in the twenties and in Italy in the mid-forties, film has invariably approached documentary.

The reassertion of political and social questions ignored in the films of Antonioni, Fellini (from *La Dolce Vita,* 1960), Alain Resnais and Bergman, coincided with the aesthetic impasse reached by each of these directors, an impasse apparent in the deadness of Antonioni's *Red Desert* (1964), the pointless flamboyance of Fellini's *Satyricon* (1969) and the utter failure of Resnais' *Je t'aime, Je t'aime* (1969).

Directors who retained an experimental approach to their art searched for a new form, moving as far as possible from narrative modes restricted to insular traumas of the individual sensibility. In many ways Resnais anticipated the fictional documentaries with three of his films: *Hiroshima, Mon Amour* (1959), *Muriel* (1963) and *La Guerre Est Finie* (1965). But it was an abortive attempt because Resnais could not take the decisive step toward documentary. This was a pre-condition for the realization of his subject – the aftermath of the Spanish Revolution and the quest of its supporters for viable modes of commitment. Robbe-Grillet's own argument in *Pour Un Nouveau Roman* is apposite: new questions demand new forms.

The fictional documentaries toward which Resnais had made one tentative gesture before lapsing into a long period of inactivity are predominately political in scope because the internationalism of the directors participating in this "movement" is one of the sources of its vitality. These men pursued a conjunction of political and aesthetic innovation in their films and worked in conscious defiance of the dramas of ennui which had dominated cinema during the early sixties.

Their first response was to differentiate their work aesthetically from such films as *L'Avventura* (1960), *La Dolce Vita* and *Last Year at Marienbad* (1962). The few recent examples of the fictional documentary which are apolitical derive nonetheless from the aesthetics of the new films, but, like the American *Derby* (1971), they are overwhelmed by their essential pointlessness. All the successful new fictional documentaries share the effort to transcend national culture or the atomized and unrelieved preoccupation with the personal. Their art is epic because both their politics and their aesthetics treat the interaction of individual lives with the vast social conflicts and historical processes of the age.

On Native Grounds

Despite the civil rights struggles and a large student anti-war movement in the 1960s, the fictional documentary has not flourished in the United States. Films emanating from the Hollywood industry have long been controlled by bankers and large conglomerates reluctant to finance works which challenge the status quo by so much as intimating irresolvable social conflict. Hollywood will countenance a film like *Sounder* (1972), concerned with the lives of poor blacks in the South during the Depression, but only by softening and muting its subject, taking two steps back for each step forward. By relinquishing the impulse toward documentary, the film "whitewashes" and sentimentalizes its characters and their condition through the use of stock figures. There is the "good" white lady and the solitary black teacher who, by her lone efforts, lifts her pupils out of poverty and a diminished sense of self. It is, of course, an old, sad story.

Politically coherent film directors in the United States have been few. Those blacklisted during the McCarthy period had long abandoned that belief in the viability of political action which denotes the great directors of the fictional documentary. *The Go-Between* (1971) of Joseph Losey and the recent work of Dalton Trumbo, including the adaptation of his novel, *Johnny Got His Gun* (1971) bear this out.

By the late thirties the betrayal by Stalin of the Spanish Civil War had been recorded in Orwell's *Homage to Catalonia,* and delineated by Trotsky, Victor Serge and others. The purge trials dissolved most intellectual rationalizations for Stalin's police state. The Hitler-Stalin pact disabused all but the most mindlessly servile of any residual illusion that the Soviet Union pursued revolutionary or socialist aims.

Confronted by the appalling realities of the Communist movement in which they had invested so much expectation, allegiance and hope, American intellectuals scattered, depleting the Left in the United States. They divorced themselves for a long time to come from the compelling political questions which had so engaged them during the previous decade. Important figures such as Dwight Macdonald, Edmund Wilson, Mary McCarthy or Richard Wright retreated to a vague anarchism or a tired liberalism which embraced shibboleths about American society disguising in turn *its* realities of power. Others, like John Dos Passos and Sidney Hook, became witch-hunters and professional apologists for corporate capitalism. Another old sad story.

This process deprived the United States of a critically daring intelligentsia. Had a viable socialist or radical movement existed alternative to the official Communist Party, this cultural disintegration might have been avoided. The Trotskyist movement could not overcome the fact that Stalin's Russia, a giant state power controlling subservient communist parties internationally, falsely appeared to apologist and opponent alike as a Marxist society. Trotskyist and other Marxist critics suffered accordingly an isolation which was intensified, first by the New Deal's co-option of a potential radical movement and later by the cultural catatonia brought about by the Cold War.

In Europe things were different. There the communist parties had not completely dissolved the mass movement, despite leading it into political institutions of liberal capitalism. The Stalinism of the mass communist parties of Italy and France also repelled their respective intelligentsias, but their large working class base continued by its presence to pose the issue of social alternatives. Hence when Stalin's death and the worker rebellions in East Germany and Hungary made their impact on Western Europe, communist intellectuals were able to respond.

In the United States, however, the Communist movement had been so small, and its capitulation to the New Deal so complete, that no political party or movement alternative to capitalism had been able to emerge. The labor movement failed to develop its own political medium. The broad population had been left by default to the ideological blandishments of official culture. No film art comparable to that in Europe has been able to emerge in the United States from this vacuum. At best derivative, the socially conscious cinema in America (for example, the documentaries of Frederick Wiseman) has not found its formal or aesthetic basis even as radical views are without a coherent constituency in the broad population. The previous generation of radical intellectuals had left behind it no heritage upon which younger artists and thinkers could build.

Occasionally in the United States, given the range of material for a political filmmaker, a film appears which seems appropriate to the genre of the fictional documentary. *The Godfather* (1971), for example, might have moved beyond its fictional myth to explore the close connections and affinity between the Mafia and corporate capitalism. It became clear, however, that there was no room within official American filmmaking for such ideas to emerge.

Nonetheless, this had been at least Marlon Brando's original conception of the film:

> I think the tactics the Don used aren't much different from those General Motors used against Ralph Nader . . . the American government does the same thing for reasons that are not much different from those of the Mafia. And big business kills us all the time — with cars, and cigarettes and pollution — and they do it knowingly.[4]

None of these ideas emerge in Coppola's film, as they might have had Costa-Gavras accepted the assignment. Although he refused on the ground that he was too unfamiliar with the culture to achieve an authentic portrait of the Mafia, he could have done no worse than Coppola, who strove to identify with the Mafia rather than attack it, fearing even to offend a nonofficial established power. Coppola aggrandized the hero played by Brando, rendering him a mythic, all-powerful and half-seductive father figure. The conception of the character of the Don consequently makes a critique of the Mafia impossible, even had this been the director's intentions.

There is invariably a radical impulse underlying the great fictional documentaries. The desire to pose the need for an entirely new social order, common to this genre, continues to intimidate the American director who wishes to achieve wide distribution for his films. The American film itself has long been at an impasse anyway, its comedies inanely repeating themselves so that the hit of 1972, *The Heartbreak Kid,* is, for example, but a banal remake of the dated *Goodbye, Columbus* (1969). It is not

---

[4] *Newsweek,* March 13, 1972.

surprising that even when an American director does treat the same subjects as the European makers of the political fictional documentary, the result is not comparable to *The Conformist* (1970) or *The Damned* (1968). Instead we have one-dimensional melodramas like *All The King's Men* (1949) or *A Face In The Crowd* (1956) which <u>fix responsibility for injustice on deranged or misguided individuals rather than on social systems, dominant values or institutions</u>.

Toward a Political Psychology

Directors of the fictional documentary do not accept that the overtly political nature of their film must by definition entail denial or trivialization of that psychology of response at which the finest art has always been adept. Several of the recent films about fascism involve a merging of psychology and politics. *The Conformist* undertakes its study of fascism precisely through a surreal glimpse of its hero whose individual erratic behavior recapitulates the psychological dynamic which drove so many of the Italian and German middle class into the arms of leaders like Mussolini and Hitler, who offered transient relief from self-hatred and guilt.

The broad satire of Petri in both *Investigation Of A Citizen Above Suspicion* (1970) and *The Working Class Goes To Heaven* (1972) is in mockery of the institutions of the bourgeois state. The pretense that police protect citizens or that factories provide livelihood is exposed by Petri, who depicts the subjugation such institutions enforce. But the police force and the assembly lines are perceived anew through the hysteria and insanity they visit upon their victims.

In the fictional documentary at its best, psychology is not subsumed under ideology. When this has occurred in political art, the result has been empty and false – in the film as in literature. When they are most successful, fictional documentaries render the relationship of personal experience to the social order so subtly that the work reproduces at once a milieu and the individuals whose values typify it. Several of these films draw upon the neo-realist beginnings of Vittorio De Sica and Roberto Rossellini.

When the interconnection between psychology and social experience is forced or is more theoretical than achieved, what results may be interesting failures, like Makavejev's *W. R. Mysteries of the Organism* (1971). Milena, his heroine, believes in "free love," which she attempts to act out with a frigid Soviet iceskater who visits Yugoslavia. But how the Russian's inability to accept her love (he murders Milena with his ice skate) is connected to the anti-Stalinist intimations in the film is unclear. The director assumes a necessary relation between sexual and social liberty, but his "situations" function as mere assertions of this fact, rather than as demonstrations of it.

Toward an Audience

The audience appeal of these films frequently results from their search for causality — their exploration of political questions to which their audiences have not yet found adequate answers. Several have explored what it is that draws men to fascism and why movements created in the name of those oppressed have failed or have been betrayed.

If Arthur Koestler's *Darkness At Noon* expressed in fiction the nightmare of a generation about the implications of Stalinism, Costa-Gavras attempts the same form of mythic statement in *The Confession,* based upon the autobiography of Artur London. If the film is denied the magnitude of Koestler's work, it is because the audience is given no more insight into Artur London's trauma than was the reader of his book. But the questions themselves, of consequence even to people who have not lived them, continued to be relevant to anyone interested in the history of the Communist movement: Why would a loyal party functionary who questioned nothing be condemned by the very party in whose name he has fought all his life? How radical and humane were this party's objectives and practices, as distinct from its pretenses? What went wrong and why?

Czechs, whose experience now recapitulates that of London, have no chance to see *The Confession,* and it is unlikely that this situation will change in the near future. The problems of London are never shown to the people who have lived them. Because these fictional documentaries often do not reach those whose experiences they depict, they appear to appeal to audiences far smaller than those attracted to *The Godfather* or *Love Story* (1970). This is misleading. *Sweet Sweetback's Baadasssss Song* (1971) says more to blacks than *The Godfather,* even as *The Confession* does to Czechs or to Russians. *Cabaret* (1972) had to be cut to be shown in Germany today, forty years after the rise of Hitler, *because* of the size of an audience for whom the film evoked its own past. It is an inverted measure of the potential appeal of many fictional documentaries that those in power in countries in which they are set ban their appearance. *W.R.* bears this out. Dusan Makavejev has now been indicted in Yugoslavia on the criminal charge of "derision," a development which might have been written derisively by Makavejev himself.

Audiences, beyond those whose experiences are directly conveyed in these fictional documentaries, are often students disturbed by oppression and war, and susceptible to art concerned with the nature of power. Many of these directors lament the systems of distribution which prevent their work from reaching the audiences for whom they were made. Bertolucci has stated: "When you do a revolutionary film ... it never goes into a revolutionary space. It goes into festivals. So you do a revolutionary film for the cinephiles, the people who like movies ... all films which are made within the system are also exploited by the system."[5]

This in part is why Godard has so single-mindedly devoted himself to films whose rhetoric and opacity render them unacceptable to commercial art cinemas; he tends, perversely, to regard restriction as a badge of radical merit, although he has not been adverse to entering his films in festivals. But apart from his fear of being absorbed, Godard makes his films for initiates. Replete with slogans, didactic voice-overs and cartoon-like images, they can only engage those whose political direction may allow "reshaping," but who share Godard's central premises.

Art and Ideology: Godard and Pontecorvo

Godard's prime justifications for films which center on harangue amount to special pleading. A film can fail to get distribution not

---

[5] Personal conversation in Rome, May, 1972.

only because it is radical, or because of its "documentary" quality, but because it is ill-conceived or dull. Nor, by invoking commercial failure, can Godard automatically earn acceptance of poor art on grounds of radical intent. From Eisenstein to Brecht, revolutionary art has been widely accessible, dramatic in form and not at all dependent upon the declamation of homilies.

Revolutionary art, on the contrary, has as its task cathartic evocation of experience surrounded in the old order by ignorance or misconception. It is through facing us with the ways in which we are used unawares and to our moral and personal detriment that new perception can arise through bold art. In this sense, all great art should be revolutionary and human drama its proper subject. Godard caricatures revolutionary sentiment by intoning, instead of creating credible feelings in the concrete experience of living people.

His most recent film, *Tout Va Bien* (1972), stars Yves Montand and Jane Fonda. But its crude satire (striking workers lock the manager in his office and refuse to give him permission to urinate), can engage only those still predisposed to approve Godard's failed quest for a mode or style in film which itself expresses the political and intellectual conceptions he wishes both to articulate and to vindicate. Paradoxically, by moving closer to a crude, almost amateur *cinema verité*, Godard has sacrificed those fictional elements in his films which would allow his documentary purpose psychological credibility and causal coherence. In his work we have evidence of how fictional documentary as a form and a style is necessary. The concern with actual events revitalizes cinema, and the fictional creation of complex experience prevents flat, dreary visual citation of the obvious, which is characteristic of the movietone newsreel of the forties and of Godard's didacticism of the seventies.

Tout Va Bien closes with an inscription: "A tale for the foolish who still need one." Godard began his career with the *nouvelle vague* in the early sixties by abolishing narrative, becoming the most interesting filmmaker of them all. In his current Maoist phase, he flouts all expectations his audience has of a formal sophistication which would integrate his didactic political imperatives with cinematic concerns. For all this, his approximation of the fictional documentary is unique, even as his conception of militancy remains unshared by other political filmmakers.

Pontecorvo, for example, would not conceive *The Battle of Algiers* as a surrogate lecture. To him an acid test of the value of his work is appreciation by people uninterested in politics at all. Those uninvolved with the F.L.N. are engaged by the film because through its treatment and themes emerges a drama about hope and the great deceptions which have plagued human beings.

Pontecorvo refuses to lead the audience by sentimentalizing the Algerians, striving instead to present the passion and suffering of the Algerian revolution truthfully. He offers a complex view of the Para colonel, Mathieu. French colonials and Algerians alike are portrayed locked by large historical developments into roles which they must play to their conclusions. This historicity of his film was for Pontecorvo an important reason for showing the French as people caught up in villainy – rather than focusing on a single villain – even as he captured the passion of the Algerian populace for independence from the colonial master. Individual natures, including those of oppressors, are less Pontecorvo's focus than is the logic of the social forces which envelope and define them.

Pontecorvo wished to approximate *cinema verité* and to convince people who knew little of Algeria of the truth of his representation. He turned to the techniques of television cameramen. He photographed much of his film with a telephoto lens as television newsmen must do, placed as they are far from actual combat zones. No dollies were used. The camera was hand-held throughout, further shortening the distance between spectator and action. *The Battle of Algiers* is the most successful of the fictional documentaries because Pontecorvo reproduced so meticulously the moment of actual battle. He sought from the audience an empathy derived from "being there," from experience rather than information.

Yacef Saadi, the co-producer of the film, played his life role as military commander of the zone of Algiers. His nephew portrayed the thirteen-year-old revolutionary, "le petit Omar." The set for the house of the terrorist Ali La Pointe was built on the site where Ali was actually blown up. Although this was fortuitous, as it was the only spot in the crowded Casbah suitable for the construction of a set, the discovery reflects the authenticity of Pontecorvo's approach. The film is a model of that political art in which values flow from the internal necessities of an action, at once credible and inexorable. It is the greatest measure of the film's aesthetic integrity that while it emulates the experience of newsreel, including voice-over commentary, it never intimates the didactic.

Godard and Pontecorvo are at opposite points in the fictional documentary. Evoking our era of social confusion in which people grope for a coherence no longer accessible within the traditional social order, Godard and Pontecorvo have each forged a unique style commensurate with their sense of the nature of that quest. But while Pontecorvo evokes many probing questions, all posed but unanswered, such as the fate of a revolution after independence, Godard propounds self-evident political maxims.

The insistence on the part of Godard's narrators that they search for truth is disingenuous. The recent *Letter to Jane* (Fonda) putatively addresses the question of the "role intellectuals play in the revolution." In fact, the conclusions are known all along and the film sacrifices the search for truth characteristic of the fictional documentary at its best. In *Letter to Jane* (1972) the frequent occurrence of Godard's voice over a blank screen with no image to distract us is the ultimate — not in engaged cinema, but in the non-film, possessing neither fictional interest nor documentary credibility. The movie consists predominantly of the image of Jane Fonda photographed in North Vietnam. Cinema is returned to its origins in still photography, and it becomes legitimate to doubt whether Godard is any longer involved in film at all.

Unlike Pontecorvo, Godard, wholly distracted by his desire to state received truths, no longer explores the potential of the camera. But this "approach" is tolerable only to those unaware or uncaring of how minds alter. It is, therefore, self-serving and a rather embarrassing presumption for Godard to assert that a "film" with no moving pictures, like *Letter to Jane,* can "help the Vietnamese win their independence." Through a convoluted voice-over, Godard dwells insultingly on the thought that Jane Fonda's efforts in North Vietnam are perforce counterproductive. This is supported by the contrivance of noting how in a widely published photograph used on the cover of *Paris-Match,* Fonda is in sharp focus while an anonymous Vietnamese in the background is indistinct, blurred for Godard into insignificance. Fonda's distraught expression on viewing bombing victims is compared to other photographs – of her father, Henry, or of Nixon looking pensive or similarly distressed. Godard proceeds to scorn the value of the actress's political activities because the attention to her emotion is interchangeable with that of other "personalities," presumably obscuring the Vietnamese *per se.*

Such logic is offensive to audiences, with its suggestion that the attention given Fonda's advocacy, or that of Sartre, renders Vietnamese suffering less immediate. It should go without saying that human grief or discomfort are expressed facially in similar ways by different people, and that neither the people nor the cause of their distress are thereby assimilated. Such straining underlines the default which Godard brings to his work. He evades the aesthetic problem of developing a style appropriate to political reality by his denial of the necessity. He may well be asked why it is not as effective to photograph the pages of a written tract and flash them in sequence on a screen.

Godard avoids the issue of how cinema as an art form is able to engage an audience at a level of deep unconscious feeling, while at the same time serving conscious aesthetic and conceptual ends. He argues that while the Vietnamese figure is in the background "like an extra," Jane Fonda, whatever her asserted beliefs, represents "the capitalist machine with cynical humility." But his rhetoric is so enclosed, and, paradoxically, so private, that the clear effect is neither provocative nor exploratory. It is hard to believe that at some level he did not know this or he would have filmed Jane Fonda's response, instead of inviting an absent Fonda to reply.

In other examples of Godard's contribution to the fictional documentary through the exhortatory mode, fiction is finally abandoned in favor of ideology. In quest of the objective, by satisfying himself with assertion, Godard's work becomes so subjective that it comes full circle and loses the documentary spirit, even as it simultaneously loses the fictional.

Costa-Gavras' finest suspense melodramas, *Z* and *The Confession,* contain many of the faults Godard has sought to avoid or transcend. Selecting historical events of considerable complexity which demand political insight, Costa-Gavras reconstructs them as adventure films replete with chases, murders and detective-story plots. They reveal only incidentally and marginally the structure of the societies he presents, despite his aspiration to do so. Because Costa-Gavras is ambivalent about an intellectual break with the politics of the official Communist movement and is confused about the premises from which a Marxist would derive this differentiation, *The Confession* is a far less integrated film than *Z* with its clear revulsion for the vicious politics of the Greek fascist regime. Costa-Gavras is not as imaginative as Godard, who is invariably inventive when he allows his flair for technique to carry his political sensibility.

Godard's intercuts, for example, of street excavations in *Two or Three Things I Know About Her* (1966) convey succinctly the rape of Paris by a technology in the service of the profit motive. His characters pursue their lives unmindful of the steady destruction of their environment. At one point Godard pans 360 degrees around one of his heroines as she stands talking to us on her balcony; meanwhile we perceive just beyond her line of vision the death throes of a Paris Walter Benjamin had called "the capital of the nineteenth century," and Paris, of course, is the "her" of the film's title.

In *Vladimir and Rosa* (1971), another of his recent fictional documentaries, there is a vignette of Godard and Jean Pierre Gorin, his co-director and collaborator, discussing revolutionary art on a tennis court. The two are oblivious to the feckless game going on about them. Tennis balls are batted back and forth, but are only seen as they whisk past the two heads engaged in conversation about revolutionary aims in the midst of bourgeois indifference. The image expresses the concept and organically interrelates the fictional with the documentary.

At such moments, Godard enhances the medium and reminds us that he has been working longer with the fictional documentary (since 1966) than other directors. It is his very talent which adds pity to our dismay over his current predominant style, in which he aborts great gifts in favor of mindless literary devices and revolutionary clichés. As his trademark he has developed the travelling shot which allows the camera to move slowly across the screen parallel to the action and frequently ironic toward it. One scene of *Tout Va Bien* occurs in a gargantuan provincial supermarket where items of food, clothing and household implements are sold. An endless line of checkout counters are a visual expression of the treadmill of bourgeois life. Godard has had the Fonda figure begin to question her "historical role" and he places her in a supermarket as a microcosm of the bourgeois consumer society. There, as a newspaper correspondent, she discusses with shoppers how they feel about the society in an attempt to discover how she can hope to change it. As she moves along among the shoppers, the checkout counters become a gauntlet she is made to run before she can reach the preconceived truths outlined by Godard and Gorin in the voice-overs.

The camera tracks along just beyond the cashiers, bisecting the market. When it reaches its destination, it begins travelling back over the same area, an unusual device but useful for Godard who wishes to represent the inexorability of change. The decadent capitalist society, for which the supermarket stands as a symbol, will become extinct, Godard and Gorin imply, just as surely as the movement of the camera seems to be inevitable and beyond either hesitation or human interference.

A group of students stage a revolt against a Communist Party spokesman selling books in one of the aisles. Because the party betrayed the workers in May 1968, the students refuse to allow him to sell his books, an action with which Godard seems to be in sympathy. The camera begins to track faster as the students loot the market, encouraging the shoppers, many of whom are black, to leave without paying. It passes by the correspondent, Jane Fonda, whose progress, both political and physical, is too slow. She is thereby rendered by the camera an intellectual soon to be bypassed by history and who, as Godard has told us earlier in the film, must "rethink herself in historical terms." The critical vitality of the sequence is not sustained because Godard does not address the anomaly wherein students substitute themselves for a victimized populace as yet unprepared for revolt. This facile attempt to evade problems as huge as they are characteristic of our era, and which the genre of the fictional documentary has been equipping itself to express, condemns such work to the realm of remote abstraction.

Z and *The Confession,* however, undertake an easier task than that assumed by Godard. Police repression and attractive victims guarantee an interest less easy to achieve for the political complexities involved. Costa-Gavras' films nonetheless are more realized than Godard's because they seek dramatically to involve us in a quest for truth about the history of our time. The *raison d'être* of the fictional documentary is the search for clarity about historical issues which affect us far beyond the two hour microcosm enacted on film. These works are effective to the degree that they enrich that quest and unfold actions as if their resolution were not forced by the screenwriter or the director.

Heroes, Anti-Heroes and the Masses

Z actually becomes interesting only with the death of its nominal hero, Gregory Lambrakis (Montand), because his real views and political past are made so unspecific and opaque. When a young lawyer and an assistant prosecutor with origins deep within the Greek hierarchy begin their investigation, the film begins to grow as do these characters. Costa-Gavras displays the minutiae of fascist Greece through fascinating imagery. The journey past small shops and the docks of Salonika depicts tightly knit cliques of thugs sustained and organized by "respectable" police and by military power. Individual participants are seen through the incredulous eyes of a picture-snapping journalist, images culminating in a meeting of the fascist cabal (C.R.O.C.) intercut as a *tableau vivant.* *Z* retains its interest despite the absence of a "hero."

Fictional documentary, paradoxically, is often most dramatic when it turns away from the elements of fiction and makes use of actual events. Characterization is heightened when we recognize real individuals beyond screen personalities. The scene in *The Confession* most revealing of the workings of the Czech bureaucracy occurs in the courtroom. Accused of unspecified crimes by a regime which he has served for fifteen years, Artur London (Yves Montand) discovers he is but one of fourteen defendants, all former colleagues in the government. Intercut with accusations against him are flashbacks in which London voted in support of the Rajk trials in Hungary, participating in the daily workings of the very government now persecuting him.

The film moves back and forth between individual lives and historical detail, alternating their importance. The grim absurdity of the courtroom scene is expressed by Costa-Gavras in a comic moment relieving extreme tension, one in which history yields to the eccentricities of personal behavior. The trousers of one of the defendants, Otto Sling, drop to the floor as he is being questioned (an actual incident). Joining in with the others' laughter, Sling, in his pathos, becomes as much the film's center as does London. The more London is perceived as a limited narrator with a flawed understanding of what is happening to him, the more effective the film becomes, both politically and artistically.

An "unreliable" hero places, however, a special responsibility on the director to clarify issues by means other than the (inadequate) perceptions of his central character. The problem with the conclusion of *The Confession* is that only a bewildered London views the Soviet invasion of Czechoslovakia in 1968, appalled but still incredulous. Costa-Gavras himself, by remaining distant from the action, similarly inhibits any illumination of the social and political nature of either the Soviet Union or its handful of Czechoslovak oligarchs. They torture, imprison and frame men who had given a lifetime of service to this party, labelling *them* traitors while their country is invaded. Costa-Gavras never offers to London a rational hint of the class character of the Party or the causes of its betrayal of socialism, a dimension central to Koestler's novel and to political coherence in the film.

Bertolucci is more successful in conveying the historical meaning of the period in *The Conformist* because his mise-en-scene is not dependent upon the character of Clerici, the Oedipal fascist at the center of the film. Our sympathies with Clerici, as with his politically impotent, anti-fascist Professor Quadri, are so filtered by awareness of their failings that we can see character in this film as a metaphor embracing the entire spirit of Italian fascism. Bertolucci makes his own perceptions apparent through a dramatization of the insufficiencies of his people confronting a crucial moment in history.

The fictional documentary often functions best without a hero as its center, as in *The Battle of Algiers*. Ali La Pointe disappears by the middle of the film and is a minor figure in it, despite the drama surrounding his fate. Pontecorvo chooses to interest us more in Colonel Mathieu and in the F.L.N. leader, Larbi Ben M'hidi, who perceives that as difficult as an armed revolution is to develop and sustain, it will be still more difficult to build a new society out of the ashes of the old. The film thus focuses on character only when a particular person or identity bears a truth relevant to that segment of the action. When the moment passes, he recedes again into the background. Pontecorvo has described this method: *"Les personnages émergeront quelques minutes dans la lumiere pour être aussitot réabsorbés par la masse."*[6] (The individual characters will emerge for a few moments only to be reabsorbed swiftly into the mass.)

Pontecorvo has been criticized for making the French too appealing in his characterization of Colonel Mathieu, who half jokes about Sartre joining his side. He is witty, appealing and cosmopolitan, despite being a torturer. An audience can sympathize less with the Algerians at such moments. It must contrast a physically vibrant, philosophical and shrewd Mathieu — able to observe in the face of an adversary that "he is not a man to make futile gestures" — with Larbi Ben M'hidi, short, retiring, with glasses and without the Colonel's panache. But it is Mathieu who uses napalm and systematic torture, while Ben M'hidi struggles in defense of his people and is tortured to death under orders of the same urbane Mathieu. The physical characteristics of the two men are poorly deployed, forcing our sympathies to be squandered and setting up a counter tension which does not so much add nuance as pointless ambiguity. It is not that the victim need be cast in a classic mold with the tormentor speaking in the hissing tones of Hollywood gestapo men. But the personae of these men are slightly out of keeping with their self-perception and their real behavior. To avoid either problem, their appearances should perhaps have been comparable.

---

[6] From an interview with Guy Hennebelle, "Une Si Jeune Paix," *Cinéama 65,* December, 1965, p. 29.

Because it is devoted so exclusively to the trial, *Sacco and Vanzetti* (1971), directed by Pontecorvo's long-time assistant and friend, Giuliano Montaldo, is wholly dependent on the characters of the two men for its clarification of the historic period. It fails precisely because, having established such dependence, Montaldo then conveys very sketchily and inadequately the personalities and lives of his two central characters.

We never learn enough to understand why Sacco and Vanzetti became anarchists or how their political commitments were integrated into the texture of their daily lives. To work well, the fictional documentary must shun equally undramatized rhetoric and the romantic hero whose presence substitutes for and obscures the historical questions at the heart of the film. As in all dramatic art, a character must be fully drawn, however limited his appearances.

This problem appears as well when the director vacillates between using nonprofessional actors who can impart a greater authenticity, and professional actors whose repute makes the film more marketable and who act with greater polish. This is particularly true when a historical film is shot on its actual location. In *Burn!* (1969), Pontecorvo's film following *Algiers,* Marlon Brando plays a nineteenth-century colonial adventurer sent to the Netherlands Antilles to suppress a guerrilla uprising. Brando's personality, including ambiguities he achieves by facial expression alone, envelops us. The revolutionary, Jose Dolores, is played by a man who had never seen a movie before he met Pontecorvo. The film's attempts to draw analogies between his situation and that of Fidel Castro are dimly realized because of the transcendant vitality Brando brings to his character. His emotional nuance is more communicative than that of Dolores, causing the audience's feelings to undermine the director's intent.

In *Joe Hill* (1971) the hero, played unwisely by a professional, Thommy Bergren, is too sweet to achieve the historical figure he portrays; sympathetic identification from the audience is cheaply achieved. Wallace Stegner, in his non-fiction novel, *The Preacher and The Slave,* is closer to the real Joe Hill, who had to be harder and more severe to have lived the organizer's life. The angelic lad given us by Widerberg is charming, but implausible.

A Case in Point: Joseph Losey's Trotsky

Unlike the fictional documentaries in which Brando stars, Joseph Losey's *The Assassination of Trotsky* (1972) does not fail because a romantic hero obscures and displaces the clarification of social conflicts. Richard Burton is a stolid, pedantic, scarcely breathing, barely believable Trotsky. The film itself virtually suggests the fictional documentary in a state of artistic exhaustion and decline.

The quest for a fresh view of historical events, which continue to plague us because we have not come to terms with them, is utterly absent from this film. When experience of the past has been reified into misleading cliché and dogma, as in the case of official views of Trotsky, openness about what has, wrongly, been taken for granted should be liberating. The rediscovery, for example, of fascism as a phenomenon requiring new perceptions of its psychological and social roots, accounts for the fascination with Bertolucci's *Conformist* in its exploration of the fascist era in Italy. It is true as well of Carlos Saura's *The Garden of Delights* (1970) which locates the ascendance of Franco in a surrealist vision of a typical household of the Spanish oligarchy.

What is lacking in Losey's *Assassination of Trotsky* is the desire for truth so characteristic of the fictional documentary at its finest. Nothing is as disturbing in Losey's handsomely mounted Mexican production as the dissembling and the sense of fatigue in the director. There are sepia photographs of Trotsky as a child, as a student revolutionist at the time of his first arrest, as a founder of the Red Army and in exile. They clearly situate the film in the realm of fictional documentary, but do little to raise the questions we have come to associate both with the genre and with the figure of Trotsky. As with Pontecorvo and Costa-Gavras, Losey's premise is that through fictionalizing history, we reexperience it more authentically than through long, familiar newsreel footage with preconceived meanings. Pontecorvo's work established that the fictionalization of history through the *mode* of the newsreel achieved greater credibility in the fictional documentary than the newsreel footage itself. The sole reason that the newsreel footage in *Sacco and Vanzetti* is effective at all is that the fictional aspects of the film are themselves so inadequately realized.

Losey's film illustrates how the premises of the fictional documentary can be abused. The failure of *The Assassination of Trotsky* results from Losey's fear of his nominal subject. The fictional documentary which evades the history it purports to treat must be moribund and is likely to bore. Losey, clearly unemancipated from his own Stalinist past, purges Trotsky from his troubled mind by creating a stiff, unreal man.

We are presented with the same grotesque distortion of Trotsky long invented by the official Communist movement. He becomes an irresponsible fanatic who sacrificed the revolution in power to pursue pseudo-revolutionary aims through instant, premature and random insurrections. The G.P.U. man shown arguing that replacing Stalin's government will result in fascism in the U.S.S.R. is sensible, practical and possessed of a common sense lacking in the isolated pedant invested by Losey. We are meant to identify more with Stalin's agent than with the Trotsky who, in 1940, is quoted out of context in justification of the suppression of the sailors of Kronstadt: "Civil war is not a school for humane behavior." Nor is the audience intended to take very kindly to the callousness of another misplaced Trotsky maxim: "The great tragedies in the world will work for us." To his followers, shocked by the Nazi-Soviet pact, Losey's Trotsky scornfully remarks, "hysteria and Marxism are irreconcilable," a gross deception by Losey implying Trotsky's support for it. With these distortions we move from the realm of the documentary to that of fiction posing as the documented, in which the hero is a caricature of a historical figure.

Fearing the difficulties in presenting a realistic Trotsky, Losey also fails to make an adequate fiction, not in terms of literary accuracy, but in terms of dramatization. We are offered an irascible old man speaking into a dictaphone which he then plays back, endlessly listening to his own voice. The fictional documentary is at its worst when it obviously seeks to "document." Invented lines, interspersed with actual writings lifted out of their appropriate contexts and spoken by Burton in a semi-voice-over, do little to engage an audience.

The documentary effect so essential to films of this genre is also absent because Losey did not solicit the comment or advice of any of the political colleagues, secretaries or bodyguards present at the assassination and still alive. Instead, Losey sought an interview with Ramon Mercader, Trotsky's assassin, alive, well and a "Hero of the Soviet Union" now living in Moscow, a fact unacknowledged in the film. Mercader insisted upon a fee of $50,000 and the stipulation that the subject of Trotsky not be discussed. Losey, perhaps unwisely, decided against seeing him, even as he avoided Trotsky's associates and friends.

This unwillingness to acquaint himself with the material has produced a film with no adequate means of assessing Trotsky. Evidence has long been ample that Mercader was a paid assassin sent by Stalin. His mother was a well-known G.P.U. agent in Spain and was with him in Mexico. It is never clear in the film why Mercader becomes an assassin, and thus Losey denies himself the means of creating a credible political psychology of personality. Mercader/Jacson is rendered a simple sadist who licks his lips in pleasure when the picador does his work at a bullfight. The elaborated gore of the scene in which the bull is butchered, later intercut with shots of Trotsky, lends a macabre ambiguity to Losey's fascination with the crazed and snorting animal in his death agony.

The Assassination of Trotsky is neither interesting fiction nor truthful documentary. Although the genre frequently searches for the causality behind historical events, Losey does not explore why Trotsky evoked such extreme wrath from Stalin's followers, symbolized in the paper mache effigy of Trotsky trampled by his enemies. In fact, Trotsky is never shown by Losey as the enemy of the bureaucratic tyranny of Stalin. His writings excoriating the destruction and betrayal of revolutionary movements never emerge, nor does Losey allow Trotsky his long acknowledged cultural accomplishments in criticism and historical analysis. Occasionally Losey relies on arbitrary documentary detail to conceal the paucity of his conception. He strews on Trotsky's desk copies of *Life* and *Newsweek* and has the camera dwell on Trotsky reading *Time,* held up as if for the camera. The implication is as dishonest as it is unmistakable. The visual declaration of Trotsky's affinity to the United States lends verisimilitude to Stalin's depiction of Trotsky as an imperialist agent and an enemy of "revolution."

A Genre in Transition

But, bad as it is, Losey's *Trotsky* does not mark a decline in the fictional documentary, despite correlative evidence that the emergent radicalism of the mid-sixties no longer inspires film-makers to pursue historical themes. The detente between Nixon, Moscow and Peking renews the truths Costa-Gavras began to explore in *The Confession* — that the struggle against capitalism and colonial subjugation will find no reliable support from the official Communist movement. The American student "radicalization" has been absorbed and diffused by the campaigns of McCarthy and McGovern, as well as by Nixon's Peace Treaty, with little to show except a demobilized movement. May 1968 in France with its worker-occupied factories diminishes in memory.

Costa-Gavras' latest film, about the Tupamaro guerrilla movement in Uruguay, *State of Siege* (1973) deals with a revolution in decline. Pontecorvo plans an historical epic centering on the life of Christ as symbolic of the collapse of a social order an an entire era (*Time of the World's End*). That he has turned to an historical period so remote and overworked, suggests lack of confidence in the politics of the present. The choice of "material" is itself a mark of abstention.

Bertolucci's most recent film, *Last Tango In Paris* (1972) possesses none of the documentary qualities of *The Spider's Stratagem* (1970) or *The Conformist*. Rooted exclusively in the present, its subject is the dynamics of sexual response and the power a man may exert through the sheer force of sexuality alone. The characters try to exist outside of history in their relationship, even outside their own personal pasts. The man (can one forget it's Brando?) insists that he and his lover avoid exchanging names. They do so only at the penultimate moment when the heroine, a colonel's daughter, shoots her paternalistic lover, who dies in a fetal position. She saw his real feeling and his need only as a threat. An accessible male, willing to share the torments of his life, does not contrast well with a man who explores various methods of forcing a woman to bend to his will. This she found exciting.

For these filmmakers of the Left, history suddenly seems at an impasse. (It will be interesting to see whether Bertolucci's projected adaptation of Dashiell Hammett's *Red Harvest* will return him to the realm of the political. His other planned film, *1900*, about a poor farmer and a wealthy landowner, contains the social dimension in its very theme.) Their latest films reflect that uncertainty or malaise, even as their earlier work expressed, through revitalized examination of past social decay, a degree of hope and an implicit readiness to engage the future in struggle. Losey's work in particular displays a depletion of sensibility and a failure to come to terms with a movement in which he was once a participant and about which his feelings are painfully unresolved.

But the recent *L'Attentat* (1972), a film written by Jorge Semprun who wrote *La Guerre Est Finie, Z* and *The Confession,* treats the kidnap-murder of Mehdi Ben Barka. It has been well-received by European critics and is an indication that the historical fictional documentary remains vital. Yves Boisset, the director, approaches assassination used as a political weapon as a motif of increasing universal significance. Boisset argues as well that his work should be judged as a fiction which causes audiences to question themselves and their relations to their own governments. His aim epitomizes the concerns of these directors who have set themselves the task of awakening audiences to their own history.

It remains true that the work of Pontecorvo, Bertolucci, Costa-Gavras and others in the mid-sixties has initiated an aesthetic for a distinct genre of the motion picture, that of the fictional documentary which partakes of the advantages accessible both to the dramatic film and to the documentary. As critics have long been aware, film has a particular affinity for recording social life in flux. Those now working in fictional documentary are in the process of rediscovering and revitalizing a mode which may yet generate a new engaged cinema, aesthetically creative, politically daring and capable of direct bearing on our immediate lives.

3

On Student Views of Film as History

Students react enthusiastically to visual history. They recognize and appreciate the importance of film and seem to embrace it with a sigh of relief that at long last it is being accorded a place alongside the written work as a transmitter of knowledge. Apparently recognizing its potential long before the professor, they respond readily to its use.

In the various courses I have given in which films serve as the major document for study and analysis, I find that the students emphatically agree that they are the most valuable input into the course. This observation of a student on an evaluation form for one of the film-centered history courses was repeated in numerous variations by a large majority: "The course helped me to actually see how the common people in Latin America live. You can read millions of books on the subject, but they don't become real for you until you visually see it." The students often comment that viewing Latin American societies, particularly through the eyes of Latin American filmmakers, enhances and enlarges their own perception.

Proof of the interest aroused by films is the lively discussions they engender among the students. In fact, such film-inspired discussions – and these must be taken in the context of the reading assignments and lectures that precede the viewing of the films – are the most animated my teaching assistants and I can remember. The obvious conclusion is that films elicit much more verbal response from students than books usually do. Students seem more willing to form, defend, and debate their opinions in courses in which film has served as a primary document than they customarily are in other history courses based entirely on lecture and reading.

The preceding chapter contained two scholarly efforts to conceptualize the use of film by the historian. This one contains a sampling of student response to the use of the film in history courses. The short essays by UCLA undergraduates are impressionistic, based largely on reaction to viewing films. In most of them the students relate the film to their concepts of historiography. As such, they provide a small but significant insight into how the student conceives the usefulness of film to history.

As a group these four essays affirm the potential of film for the study of history. In the first essay, Beth August ranges over broad aspects of the use of film, illustrating how a series of films can depict the life-styles of Brazilian peasants. She urges historians to take up filmmaking rather than to continue their criticism of the lack of historical approach among filmmakers. Bill Taylor emphasizes some of the similarities between the historian and the documentary filmmaker. He employs a series of five films on Bolivia to demonstrate how the film can provide an awareness of continuity, even in this case study where a major revolution would seem to have broken such continuity. The last two essays exemplify the type of critique I encourage the students to make of the films they have seen in class. The idea is to analyze the film as an historical document, answering first the simple question of how the film contributes to the better understanding of a people, culture, area, era, or event. In two such critiques – and rather typical ones at that – of *Blood of the Condor*, Bil Wadum and Magi Fainer reveal what that fictional documentary says to them and what it means to them. In interpreting that complex fictional documentary, they consider, among other things, some of the major contemporary problems of Indo-America.

Film for the Historian

BETH AUGUST

Intellectuals have shown reserve, if not outright skepticism, about the validity of documentary film as an historical source. The hesitation to use film as a reliable source has centered on conservative and static arguments.

The most important source for the historian has been the written word. Historians argue that a film, unlike a book, is harder to document and is more easily accepted as being true (seeing is believing) because there is little time to stop, analyze, and reflect on the quickly moving images shown on the screen. Some intellectuals feel that documentary film has a false sense of objectivity because of the way in which the visual image is used (editing, angle of camera, and so on), which can distort reality. It is believed that in most cases the film is used for propaganda effect and tends to oversimplify complex questions and problems because of lack of time and space. Others contend that watching a film is a passive experience – just sit back, watch, and listen – whereas reading a book requires more intellectual activity. The most telling criticism the historian can make against the validity of the documentary film is that the filmmmaker usually is not a trained historian and sometimes is interested less in the actual treatment of reality and more in the film's marketability.

Many of these objections are not fair since they apply with equal validity to books. The arguments above fall into the error of supposing that a written document or record is objective and pure and cannot persuade in one way or another the mind of the historian and the students confronting it, whereas film has a special, peculiar quality that prejudices the mind if it is not carefully viewed. All forms of documents, written or visual, must be carefully questioned.

The difficulties for historical purposes which are presented by film are not necessarily special and peculiar to film, nor are they much greater than difficulties that arise in relation to the use of other types of evidence. A film can be documented, and greater efforts are being made to facilitate that process. Why should not the historian treat film material the same as he would written evidence? The question of filmic validity should be dealt with just as one treats the written document. If a person has little prior knowledge of a subject, he should not consider any document – be it a film or a book – as being the complete truth. The individual who sees a film or reads a book does not do so with a blank mind on which any information may be projected; the individual already has built-in interpretive patterns with attitudes and beliefs that compose his psychological makeup. The "blank mind" conception of the communication process is in part responsible for much of the popular concern about the presumed "bad" or "good" effects of film.[1] It implies the existence of a mass mind unable to decide what or what not to believe and easily swayed by propaganda techniques. Propaganda is found just as frequently in other sources, so why should a person not be as questioning when he sees a film as when he reads a book?

A sequence or montage has all the bias and objectivity of a single written document. The positioning of the camera and the editing reflect the judgments and views of the times as well as those of the filmmaker. It is important to know who the filmmaker is, as it is to know the author, and to know what his background is, and the meaning and purpose of his work.

The argument has been raised that watching a film is a passive experience. Eugene McCreary and some historians would disagree with that opinion. Not only is the present student generation living in an age where the visual image has been the principal source of information and entertainment but also their psychological intake system is programmed for the moving image.[2] Therefore, most students are receptive to what film has to offer. On the other hand, because of the frequency and nature of the programs viewed, usually for entertainment purposes, intellectual analysis may be turned off. It is important for the student to have an awareness of what is to be viewed and to have questions ready in order to heighten the intellectual experience. Eugene McCreary believes that the film experience is not passive in that the eye must work subconsciously to make the motion necessary to perceive the images. Because the screen is light and everything else is dark, the eye concentrates on the lighted area from which it is hard to wander. The spectator is in constant "sensory stimulation"

---

[1] Franklin Fearing, *Motion Pictures as a Medium of Instruction and Communication* (Berkeley: University of California Press, 1950), p. 101.

[2] Eugene C. McCreary, "Film and History: Some Thoughts on Their Interrelationship," *Societas,* II (Winter, 1971), p. 51 (see p. 48, above).

possessing neither the time nor the opportunity to stop the film to reflect and using each moment to concentrate on and register information. Experiments conducted to test the effectiveness of the use of film in the learning process concluded that students retain more information for a longer time after having seen a film. They seem to learn faster and comprehend more by relating to visual images rather than to written words.[3]

The film's uniqueness is its ability to capture visual reality and act as a recorder and preserver of those images. It is a reflector of changing social attitudes and values and can act to motivate future change. Film has tremendous educational potential: more people see films than read books.

With the growing recognition of the film as a valid source of reference, more historians feel the need for documentaries to be made by qualified historians, which might eliminate much of the reluctance to accept them as historical evidence.

In April, 1968, at a conference held at the University College, London, to discuss the problems facing the historian as filmmaker, the University Historians' Film Committee was formed, with the aim of coordinating and promoting activities relating to the use of film (together with still photographs and sound recordings) for historical research and teaching. It was agreed that the producer ordinarily observes few standards of scholarship when making a film, his overriding interest being to make "an effective package and [tie] things together which may not belong together either in spirit or in time."[4] Historians want film to be historical evidence which is something that is governed by the rules made by historians. It was agreed that a historian cannot order a technician to do his history for him, so he himself must handle the camera in the way he now handles a pen.

Thus far, historians have permitted the filmmakers to do as they pleased and then criticized them for not being historical. A far more positive approach would be for the historian to become

---

[3] Fearing, *Motion Pictures*, p. 103.

[4] Patrick Griffin, "Film, Document and Historian," *Film and History*, Vol. II, No. 2 (May, 1972), p. 1.

involved in the making of films. The truth is he can no longer afford to neglect them.

Most of the older films on Latin America in the UCLA Media Library provide ample evidence of well-intentioned filmmakers ignorant of Latin American history, languages, peoples, and customs producing films about that area. (The notable exception is Julien Bryan.) Other film libraries contain similar material. Many of these films were made in the 1940s when travel films or travelogues were gaining popularity, and they are characterized by the banal images and trite narration typical of travel films. Most of the films on Latin America were made either by amateur travelers with camera equipment or by governmental agencies in conjunction with the host country, for purposes of propaganda or tourism rather than to educate or inform. The content of these films in most cases was oversimplified and stereotyped — trying to cover too much material in too little time. Most showed the North American way as being typical of the Latin American life-style so that the traveling American could be secure in his adventures into "semi-different" cultures. Most of the films depicted only the affluent (Americans could identify with this); it was therefore a biased point of view.

A trained historian will find some value in the old documentaries, since the filmmaker was obviously influenced by the values and views of his time and has reflected them in his film. The visual image in itself, no matter what the quality of the film, is important to the historian as a recorder of life and attitudes, an important point to analyze when the historian or student studies a film.

Other nonfictional documentaries not of the travelogue type also evinced such problems as the visual image projecting a different story from the narration, shallow and insensitive narration, and inferior visual images and editing because the filmmaker did not really know or understand Latin America.

More recently Latin Americans have been making their own films which merit our attention. Not only is there more sensitivity toward the subject matter but also there seems to be a more objective treatment of reality. Many films from Latin America today raise excellent questions on social issues and reflect changing social attitudes and values. Some might be able to act as a motivating force for future change. These films may be categorized into what Joan Mellen calls the fictional documentary. For the student of Latin America, these films can provide important insight into the realities of the area. For example, if a student wished to study about the life-styles and possible alternatives in northeast Brazil he could do so by using fictional and nonfictional documentaries, most of them made by Brazilians themselves. Both *The Land Burns*, nonfictional documentary, and *Barren Lives*, a fictional documentary, illustrate primarily through visual images rather than narration or dialogue the conditions under which the peasants of northeastern Brazil struggle for survival. The films provide excellent material for the researcher in that he visually can examine the cycles of poverty and determine the basic attitudes and emotions of the peasants in the framework of their life-style. The movies touch on alternatives to their life-style but do not deal with them in depth.

The fictional documentary *O Cangaceiro* examines one of the possible routes that the peasant can take in trying to break his cycle of poverty, banditry, an alternative life-style that was popular in northeastern Brazil in the 1930s. For the historian this film is significant because it shows reasons and motives behind the cangaceiro's existence. It explains how and why bandits serve as a symbol. Since the film was made, cangaceiro groups in the rural area have disappeared, but the film still remains as a visual recorder of the activity that depicted an important life-style in Brazil. The nonfictional documentary *Memories of the Cangaço* skillfully documents, through old newsreels and interviews, the Brazilian bandit and his motivations, backing up the validity of *O Cangaceiro*.

If the Brazilian peasant refuses to live in his misery, there is another alternative he can choose: migration. *Tropici*, another excellent fictional documentary, follows the migration process of a peasant family from the Northeast to an urban area in search of work and better living conditions. Juxtaposing newsreel clips with the story line, a cogent message is delivered: the peasant migrates from one misery to another and is still exploited and dependent.

The Given Word, fictional documentary, begins where *Tropici* ends. It shows the problems a peasant faces in the modern city. An expression of the attitudes between rural and urban sectors was one of the most useful elements that the historian could have extracted from this film.

The above films studied together show a true and logical progression of different possibilities that challenge the peasant's life-style. Through this sensitive visual dimension one can perceive the perplexing problems that face the rural poor in Brazil. As the number of Latin American filmmakers increase, the number of films available should also increase, therefore expanding the possibilities of topics one can research.

With the increase in the acceptance of the use of film as a valid source for history, more effective measures will need to be taken in the future in order to efficiently preserve, catalog, and maximize the accessibility of film. It is essential that historians involve themselves in filmmaking.

Historical Continuity through Film: The Example of Bolivia

BILL TAYLOR

For ten years I have traveled throughout the world taking pictures. The one thing that made it fun was that back of it all there was a story to tell and my pictures helped me do it. If at any time I could have told the story better with the printed word or over the radio I should have stopped telling it with pictures.

Just as a foreign correspondent might write a book on life in China or Japan, giving the background of the people and showing clearly their economic and social problems, I decided to do much the same thing with motion pictures.[1]

---

[1] Lewis Jacobs, *The Documentary Tradition* (New York: Hopkinson and Blake, 1971), p. 167.

In the above quotation, Julien Bryan brings into focus many of the issues that we, as historians interested in film, must grapple with. Of central importance is that film provides us with a unique and, until recently, relatively untouched source of information. It is unique because it does not seek, as Mr. Bryan's quote makes clear, to supplant the book, but rather to provide a new and different dimension; hence it is not an alternative resource so much as a supplementary one.

Film's uniqueness stems from the visual image it provides, and therefore it literally allows us to see the enactment of events in a manner a book does not allow. Skeptics may reply, "Yes but so often what we see in a documentary is not the event itself but a recreation of it." This may well be so; but does it matter? If we examine our roles as historians, we must come to the realization that the documentarist, whether he deals with fictional or nonfictional documentary, is often actually doing what we do: he is recording an event. If he actually records it, we can use it as a primary source. If he recreates it, as is usually the case in the fictional documentary, he provides us with a secondary, historical study. In many ways, he follows the traditions of historical research. He does so on two levels: first, he strives to recreate imaginatively the past; and second, in doing so he takes advantage of the same resources the historian does. To illustrate this point, let us listen to the words of the young Chilean filmmaker, Miguel Littin who explains: "I researched all available records of the case – public, journalistic and legal. I interviewed people who were with this man in prison; I visited the places where he spent his childhood, adolescence and later life."[2] That surely is the same procedure an historian would follow. Hence, following many of our methods, seeking our goal the filmmaker can provide us with a secondary source as important as any book. What separates him from more accepted historiography is solely the method of expression. It is time for historians to acknowledge this source and to try to incorporate it into their work.

---

[2] "Film in Chile: An Interview with Miguel Littin," *Cinéaste*, Vol. IV, No. 4 (Spring, 1971), pp. 4-5.

To illustrate how this may be done, let me use five films to examine the Bolivian social revolution of 1952-1964. Hopefully, these films will help us to understand why a revolution that has accomplished two of the major objectives called for by proponents of revolution, that is, land reform and the nationalization of the primary natural resource, tin, has failed to alter the miserable pattern of poverty which still characterizes Bolivia.

This poverty is ironic for Bolivia was once the richest colony in the New World. In colonial times silver was Bolivia's most important product. But she was so dependent upon this metal, highly prized by the Europeans, that with its disappearance much – and yet little – changed. The Bryan film *Bolivia* illustrates that change. As we look at the "ghost town" of Potosí it is explained that this was once a major city of one hundred and fifty thousand people. The city flourished so long as it could export the mineral Europe coveted. Once the mines were exhausted, Potosí was left only with a hole in the ground.

Rubber is another example this film shows of the exploitation of Bolivian resources by the developed world. Shown is the gathering of latex by the most primitive methods. It is made clear that these methods cannot keep Bolivian rubber important on the world market. Even though the industry was founded here, it has become unprofitable because of the rough terrain and poor transportation. When the world's industries found another source, they quickly abandoned the Bolivian jungles. The relationship between the industrialized nations and monoproductive Bolivia seems so clear. Yet, the process – despite its disadvantages to Bolivia – continues. The new raw product is tin. It is the next link in the continuity of the exploitation of a natural product and Bolivia's subsequent dependency. Because this industry is so vital to Bolivia, and because its nationalization was one of the major changes brought about by the revolution of 1952, let's see what the reality of the mines has been and is now as shown in the films on Bolivia.

Bryan shows the development of this industry by juxtaposing the old primitive methods with the modern methods which are now part of the Bolivian landscape. Hence, seen are old women picking up loose rocks, the use of manual crushers, and, in contrast, the modern, underground mines manned by the Indian labor. The work is difficult and coca is chewed to ease the pain. The picture of the miners in the tunnels conjures up the memory that their ancestors played the same role in the silver mines. The labor system may no longer be the forced one for which the Spaniards were infamous — the *mita* — but has the reality changed for the miners? Hardly. The living quarters shown in the film *End of a Revolution* are as cold and barren as those hundreds of years ago. But most interesting of all is that these are pictures taken in 1968. The mines have long been nationalized and thus Bolivia's major industry no longer remains in the hands of foreign capital; yet what is the reality of the situation for the miners, for Bolivia? As has already been pointed out the Bolivian miner can be seen living in quarters no better than those before the revolution. In fact, the narrator intones that wages recently had been slashed by one-half. And we are shown old women searching for ore they can sell to the government at a minimal price. Immediately we refer back to the Bryan film and we sadly acknowledge that despite the passing of over two decades and a social revolution little has changed for the miners. Their major institutional contact remains one of oppression as we see the army crush rebellion and are told five hundred miners were killed in one protest. An explanation is needed. General Rene Barrientos points out that Bolivia is a monoproducer. The nation relies totally on tin for its foreign exchange. But the cost of producing tin has reached the level that it no longer yields a profit and thus to make ends meet the government cut wages. The key is of course that tin is the third link in a chain of dependency. For while the revolution changed the hands of ownership, it did not change Bolivia's dependent relationship to the capitalist world and hence her development remains impossible.

The films vividly show us how these institutions of dependency still exist in modern Bolivia. I use the word modern because there has been modernization but a modernization within the dependent framework of the Bolivian economy. That modernization facilitates exploitation and imperialism. For example, in the Bryan film *Bolivia*, we are shown the old roads from the Altiplano to the sea which have long been used to export Bolivian metals. We are then shown that modernization has brought railroad tracks, but they lead along the same path as the old roads. In this case modernization has meant a cheaper, faster form of transportation for the exporting of metal; but it has also meant a continuation, an intensification of dependency. Hence we see a modern tool which not only aids in the continuation of Bolivian exploitation, but indeed impedes development.

This failure to develop appears again in *La Paz*, another film by Bryan. Much growth is shown in the form of new buildings, but little industry is evident. In fact, what is shown is rather small textile mills. It is pointed out that even here all machinery is imported and there is little fuel to operate them; but labor is plentiful and cheap which are the only attractions to foreign or domestic industrialists. Hence, one is left wondering toward what end does even this little development go.

This same film indicates that the dependent relationship is not just an economic one but indeed one that pervades all levels of culture. The narrator relates that at the movie theaters, "Mexican and Argentine films are almost as popular as North American films."[3] Indeed, cultural imperialism is as prevalent as economic. Jorge Sanjines illustrates such cultural imperialism in *Blood of the Condor* in a scene involving the Bolivian medical community. This scene illustrates the "aping" of American culture by a dominant yet insecure class. The location is a country club similar to one found anywhere in the United States and the occasion is the honoring of a group of Americans they seek to emulate.

Perhaps the efforts at land reform have been at the same time the most successful and frustrating. In the area of production progress is evident, though it is minimal. The increase can be noted from the dialogue of the Bryan film, *The High Plain*, as well as in *End of a Revolution*. The Bryan film notes that three-fourths of all food must be imported, while the second one observes that one-half of all food must be imported. The social reality becomes clearer through the visual image. In *The High Plain*, one views a large hacienda employing over two hundred Indian families. They

---

[3] Julien Bryan, *La Paz*, 1949, UCLA Media Library, No. 3477.

are working for a "progressive patron" or, as the dialogue refers to him, the "Potato King."[4] Our "progressive patron" demands from each Indian three days' work per week on the hacienda in return for the privilege of tending their own plots of land. In *End of a Revolution* the destruction of this type of servitude is noted by the image of a decaying hacienda house. But sadly the condition of the Indian peasant in material terms is not significantly better. His working methods and his housing remain largely as they have for centuries. The great failure which is so evident is that land redistribution is not enough. What is needed is agrarian reform to go along with this land reform. That means new tractors, improved seed, fertilizer are as necessary to reform as redistribution of land.

This paper suggests that film can contribute to research. It takes as an example the continuity in recent Bolivian history traceable and provable through five films: *Bolivia* (1946), *La Paz* (1949), *High Plain* (1949), *End of a Revolution* (1968), and *Blood of the Condor* (1968). Obviously these films record changes that have taken place over a period exceeding two decades. At the same time it is equally apparent from these same films that those changes have not altered a basic continuity.

The Fictional Documentary: Two Analyses of *Blood of the Condor*

1. BIL WADUM

In the film *Blood of the Condor,* Jorge Sanjines has realized his objective as a revolutionary filmmaker, at least to the extent of producing an effective medium that conveys the intelligence needed "to create a consciousness of liberation." This young Bolivian filmmaker has reconstructed an authentic historical situation, as perceived not by the alien scholar but rather by those persons who actually witnessed the historical events. In *Blood*, the

---

[4] Julien Bryan, *The High Plain,* 1949, UCLA Media Library, No. 3466.

viewer is presented with the problems experienced by and confronting one Indian village in Bolivia, although such problems are universal among Bolivian Indians. The film provides real insight into the problems these Indians face. Finally, the film offers an unequivocal solution to the problem. Whether the viewer agrees or disagrees with Sanjines's suggested solution is of secondary consequence. The real significance of the film is its undeniable impact.

The major problem of the Bolivian Indian is evident from the opening scene in the film. The geographic isolation of the barren Andes, which the Bolivian Indian has sought in order to preserve his culture, is symptomatic of his poverty. As with all conquered peoples, the Indians in Bolivia have been granted only that land neither needed nor wanted by their conquerors. But even in their isolation, the privacy of the Indian has been invaded. The government imposes upon the Indian a mestizo police force and a North American "Progress Corps." The functions of these two groups respectively are to suppress any antigovernment activity or impulse and to "civilize" (i.e., westernize) the Indians, while controlling the population (i.e., clandestine sterilization). Both the mestizos and the Americans appear to be mechanisms of an elite government pursuing a policy of Indian genocide, if not physically, at least culturally. The Indian is faced with the dilemma of either remaining in the countryside, in extreme poverty, or migrating to the urban centers where he must abandon his previous life-style and blend into a European environment.

With the brothers Ignacio and Sixto, Sanjines presents a dichotomy of the fate that awaits the Bolivian Indian along either path. Whereas Ignacio has chosen to remain in his natural environment, in hopes of preserving his culture, Sixto has decided to become a member of the urban labor force. But what Sixto soon realizes is that discrimination against the Indian there transcends that in the countryside. Although Sixto conforms to the dress, customs, and language of city, there is a prevailing attitude of prejudice among the non-Indians of the city which prevents Sixto from achieving any meaningful success or recognition. Essentially, Sixto is just another cog in the national elite machine, like Ignacio, destined to be consumed.

Causes of the Indians' plight are numerous. They may all be traced back, however, to foreign intervention and exploitation. The magnitude of this calculated foreign intrusion is exemplified in the scene where Ignacio's wife is bringing him into the city for medical aid. The expression on her face when she sees the city conveys a combined feeling of perplexity, fear, and amazement. She knows that this unnatural conglomeration was the result and cause of her suffering, but she just could not rationalize the city's consequences.

The foreign influences dominant in the city are accompanied by an attitude of superiority on the part of the foreigners and their national, middle-class, urban allies. I contend that it is this attitude, and not a deliberate attempt at genocide, which indicts the presence of the "Progress Corps." Symbolically the Corps performs involuntary cultural sterilization on Indian women. What can be concluded from the actions of the "Progress Corps" and their links with the Bolivian medical profession is that foreign intervention has not only developed means of exploiting the Indians of Bolivia, but that a psychological attitude has also been incorporated into the forces of exploitation. This attitude enables the elites to further exploit the Indians under the guise of benevolence. The effect of this attitude is perpetuation of the existing exploitation of Bolivian Indians.

I can appreciate Sanjines's fine effort to capture visually the history and plight of the Bolivian Indian. I also think that Sanjines has documented well the Indian problems and the causes of their problems. I must disagree, however, with Sanjines's advocacy of armed revolution as the solution to the Indians' plight. I feel that an armed revolution by the Indians against the Bolivian government would facilitate the physical genocide hitherto avoided by the Indians. This contention is based on the fact that an insurrection on the part of the Indians would have international repercussions which might prompt the intervention of the United States. Certainly it has been the policy of the United States to aid any government in the hemisphere (regardless of how oppressive that government may be) so long as it vociferously affirms an anticommunist attitude.

It is with despair that I conclude that there is probably no immediate panacea to the injustices suffered by the Indians of Bolivia, but revolutionary films such as *Blood of the Condor* may expose these injustices and catalyze the desperately needed reform. Hopefully the end result would be the emergence of a more representative Bolivian government acting in the best interest of its own people.

2. MAGI FAINER

In *Blood of the Condor*, Jorge Sanjines depicts the plight of Bolivian Indians in both rural and urban settings. The events in the film are seen from the Indian's point of view. Despite sincere attempts on the part of the Indians to either maintain their cultural heritage as communal farmers or to acculturate themselves into the city environment, they are ultimately confronted with social obstacles, foreign suppression, and government indifference. Consequently the Indians, as the film infers, face cultural extinction through forced urbanization or direct genocide. In demonstrating the social and political attitudes and actions that have caused this predicament, Sanjines vividly exposes various aspects of Indian communal life in conjunction with non-Indian influences affecting these Indian communities. The first of these is associated with the nature of closed Indian communities. The second salient aspect of reality treated in the film concerns the emergence of urban modernization in Bolivia's cities.

According to the definition of Eric Wolf and Edward Hansen in *The Human Condition in Latin America*, a closed community is characterized by a closely knit political-religious organization presided over by community leaders. In *Blood of the Condor*, it is Ignacio Mallkau who takes the role of the leader. By actively participating in communal affairs and sponsoring religious activities, he has gained considerable influence and prestige throughout his community. Only after he adequately fulfills his religious and economic obligations does he acquire authority through elections. Although Ignacio is the real, de facto governing force in his community, a government official, the intendant, represents the power of the state. Owing to the cohesive nature of Ignacio's closed community, however, he warrants distrust and is not received by the community members as their political leader. Consequently, he has to depend on Ignacio's compliance with government policies in order to affect cooperation among his followers. Ignacio is usually quick to submit to the intendant's edicts as he is acutely aware of the government's ultimate power. Still, Ignacio without doubt sets the standards for his people to follow. It is for this reason that the intendant shoots Ignacio. By punishing the leader of the community, he can set a precedent that will significantly deter the people from following Ignacio's rash example.

Another prominent closed community characteristic emphasized in the film is the distrust of outsiders. Clearly the intendant is constantly held suspect and in contempt by the Indians. This distrust of outsiders increases further with the appearance of the three Progress Corps members. They are foreigners; not only are they not Indians, they are not even Latin Americans. Furthermore, their presence eventually becomes associated with the fact that no babies have been born in the community for two years. It follows that because members of the closed community distrust outsiders, they naturally depend on members within their own society for advice or guidance. Not only is Ignacio, as the community leader, accorded sufficient respect to merit him giving advice, but also senior male members of various households are accorded this advisory position. It is easy to see, then, why Ignacio consults with his wife's family, particularly the oldest member, the grandfather, to discover why the women of the community have not borne any children.

A final factor characteristic of the closed community that Sanjines depicts in his film is the religious beliefs of the Indians. Outstanding among them is fear that an outsider, an enemy of the community, may inflict an evil spell on the community. At one point while Ignacio is seeking to discover why Paulina has not conceived a child, a community religious leader attributes the cause to a spell on the entire community causing death in the women's wombs. The community finally determines that it is the Progress Corps representatives who are responsible for the women's barrenness. The Indians of Ignacio's community also believe in various deities with power to affect their lives. Each of these deities performs a different function. Whereas Mother Coca empowers men to perceive the future, the Sun gives man knowledge.

After the intendant's men shoot Ignacio, the wounded leader is taken to his brother Sixto in the city for help. It is at this point that Sanjines turns his attention to the impact of urban modernization upon the Indian. The film demonstrates that in order for an Indian to adapt to an urban environment, he must relinquish his customs and beliefs, that is, his Indian heritage. Thus, Sixto, in his attempt to become acculturated in the city, abandons his native tongue for Spanish and ignores the deities inherent in his native religion to adopt at least the outward forms of Roman Catholicism. At one instance, while playing soccer, he even goes so far as to deny his Indian birth, demanding to know why another player has called him "Indian." Sixto is so intent on becoming a member of a Westernized society that being called an Indian is an insult — after all, as he remarks, the accusing soccer player did not see him being born. By witnessing the adamance with which Sixto denies his Indian heritage, the audience is led to assume that in reality racial discrimination prevents all Indians from securing well-paying jobs, financial loans, or any opportunity for upward mobility.

The condescending attitude of the Westernized urban society is evident in a number of scenes in the film. In the hospital, for example, the doctors treat Sixto paternally, offering him minimal and therefore inadequate advice on how to obtain the necessary blood to save his brother's life. He encounters similar insensitiveness from the wife of the clinic director, a doctor who could have been of some help to him but is more concerned with his relationship to foreign medical "experts." Apparently, because Sixto displays the physical characteristics of an Indian, the elite doctors feel that his needs cannot possibly be urgent enough to warrant interruption of their affairs.

To further illuminate the insensitive attitudes Bolivian Indians must confront, Sanjines uses the Progress Corps members. Even if these people have been genuinely sincere in their attempts to offer meaningful aid to Ignacio's community (and Sanjines implies that they were not), their success would have been limited owing to the fact that they — being foreigners with no previous knowledge of traditional communities — are not attuned to the needs of Ignacio's people. They advocate birth control to halt an increasing population in an impoverished community without taking into account the Indians' great desire to proliferate their race, their cultural value of children, and their need for family support in work. They also donate clothes to the community which can never be used, as they are indiscriminately given without consideration for size, utility, or age of the recipient, not to mention cultural values. Obviously, the Progress Corps members make these useless benevolent gestures with the expectation of eliciting great quantities of gratitude from the Indians in the community. They feel the Indians will simply appreciate their "great self-sacrifice." Owing to their lack of understanding of the Indians' desire to maintain their present culture (without the burden of forced Westernized intervention), these people also hypothesize that reducing the community's population will alleviate problems of diminishing food and shelter resources.

Although Sanjines vividly portrays the possibility of extinction among traditional Indian life-styles, he does ultimately offer a solution. This solution lies in the determination of Indians to emphasize and pursue their own unique cultural existence. The realization of this solution comes to Sixto only after Ignacio dies and he accepts the fact that he has been defeated by his urban environment. In order for the valorization of Indian culture to occur, however, the national government must be sympathetic to this goal. First, the government needs to directly support these communities, allowing them to survive without exploitation. Second, foreign intervention by such organizations as symbolized by the Progress Corps must be prohibited. Sanjines employs *Blood of the Condor* as a warning that if Sixto's efforts to rejuvenate the traditional Indian life are foiled, a social revolution will ensue.

4

In Search of Films

Finding the right films for research or the classroom is a major challenge. The search for celluloid documentation of Latin American history today must be roughly analogous to a similar quest on the part of the North American academics for the written documents two or possibly three generations ago. Scholars slowly but admirably have been solving that problem with the publication of guides to national, regional, state, local and private archives, notes on library holdings, locations of newspaper files, and evaluations of manuscript collections. Now the time has arrived to divert some of that curiosity and energy toward locating and describing film depositories.

No guide to film collections on Latin America exists. Fragments of information can be picked up from scattered references and, of course, must be pieced together. In this chapter, I suggest some starting points for the researcher, student, and teacher. The information, alas, is scant. It serves only as an orientation for future research.

The Audiovisual Archives Division of the National Archives, Washington, D.C., contains a large and important film collection. Three articles introduce the collection as well as the filmic services of the National Archives:

> Dorothy Arbaugh, "Motion Pictures and the Future Historian," *American Archivist,* II (April, 1939), pp. 106-114.
>
> William T. Murphy, "Film at the National Archives: A Reference Article," *Film & History,* Vol. II, No. 3 (September, 1972), pp. 7-13.
>
> William T. Murphy, "The National Archives and the Historian's Use of Film," *The History Teacher,* Vol. VI, No. 1 (November, 1972), pp. 119-134.

Universal Pictures has donated its newsreel collection to the National Archives. It covers the 1929-1967 period.

Guides to three major film collections in the United States — The Museum of Modern Art in New York City, George Eastman House in Rochester, New York, and the Library of Congress in Washington, D.C. — can be found in *Film Quarterly,* Vol. XVI, No. 2 (Winter, 1962-1963), pp. 35-42. That issue also contains valuable information on library resources and bibliographic and reference tools (pp. 45-50).

Professor Jane Loy compiled the addresses of the major university film collections with Latin American holdings. See her *Latin America: Sights and Sounds. A Guide to Motion Pictures and Music for College Courses* (Gainesville: Consortium of Latin American Studies Programs, 1973), pp. 225-228. Omitted from that list is the UCLA Media Library which holds an excellent collection of about sixty documentaries on Latin America made in the 1940-1960 period, a high percentage of them by Julien Bryan. Cynthia Baird prepared another useful guide: *La Raza in Films: A List of Films and Filmstrips* (Oakland, Calif.: Latin American Library, 1972). This excellent annotated filmography includes a wide variety of films on Latin America. The majority of fictional documentaries about Latin America made by Latin Americans and with English subtitles are distributed by New Yorker Films (43 West 61st Street, New York, N.Y., 10023) and the Tricontinental Film Center (P.O. Box 4430, Berkeley, Calif., 94704). Both send catalogues upon request.

Twentieth Century-Fox's footage of Movietonews, a historical collection of filmed news reportage from 1908 to the present, is now available for viewing. The footage is completely indexed and cross-referenced. The library may be reached by writing Movietonews, Inc., 460 West 54th Street, New York, N.Y., 10019.

The *AHA Newsletter* (American Historical Association) began to publish, with the May-June, 1974, issue, a section entitled "Media and History." It promises to carry news on collections available for research, projects in progress, and research grants.

An idea of the film collections in Great Britain can be gleaned from two publications:

Ivan Butler, *To Encourage the Art of the Film. The Story of the British Film Institute* (London: Robert Hale, 1971).

Colin Ford, "The National Film Archive" in *Film and the Historian* (London: British Universities Film Council, 1969), pp. 36-41.

For those doing research in Latin America, I recommend consulting the following *cinematecas* for orientation:

Argentina: Cinemateca Argentina, Lavalle 2168 – 1° – 37, Buenos Aires. Curator: Guillermo Fernández Jurado.

Brazil: Fundação Cinemateca Brasileria, Caixa Postal 12900, 04113 São Paulo. Director: Rudá Andrade.

Cinemateca do Museu de Arte Moderna, Caixa Postal 44, 2000 Rio de Janeiro. Director: Cosme Alves Neto.

Instituto Nacional do Cinema, Praça da República, 141-A, Rio de Janeiro.

Colombia: Cinemateca Colombiana, Apartado Nacional 1898, Bogotá. Director: Hernando Salcedo Silva.

Cuba: Cinemateca de Cuba, Calle 23, No. 1155, Vedado, Havana. Director: Hector Garcia Mesa.

Guatemala: Cinemateca Enrique Torres de Guatemala, Universidad de San Carlos, Guatemala City. Director: Leonel Mendes.

Mexico: Cinemateca Mexicana, Córdoba 45, Mexico 7, D.F. Director: Galdino Gómez-Gómez.

Paraguay: Cinemateca Paraguaya, Estrella 496, Asunción. Director: Oscar Trinidad.

Uruguay: Cine Arte del S.O.D.R.E., Andes y Mercedes, Montevideo. Curator: Eugenio Hinz.

Cinemateca Uruguaya, Rincon 569, Montevideo. Director: M. Martinez Carril.

Cinemateca del Tercer Mundo, Casilla de Correo 943, Montevideo. Director: Mario Handler.

In Search of Films *115*

> Venezuela: Cinemateca Nacional, Edificio Anexo al Musco de Ciencias Naturales, Plaza Morelos, Los Caobos, Caracas. Director: Rodolfo Izaguirre.

The Cineteca Nacional de México in Mexico City, inaugurated in January of 1974, is a luxuriously appointed institution with three theaters, a library, bookstore, exhibition hall, and ample office and storage facilities. For the present, it houses no newsreels and few documentaries but is collecting under its protection a majority of the commercial films made in Mexico. Its staff is busily preparing a catalog of the film collection as well as a guide to the Cineteca. Some information on the cinematecas of Latin America can be found in the Mexican film journal *Cinemateca,* numbers 1 and 2.

The challenge to search out and use the film sources for the study of Latin America is a major one. Those who accept it will propel that study in the direction it badly needs to move.

5
Bibliographies

Conceptualizing the Use of Film To Study History: A Biblio-Filmography

With increasing confidence, historians are turning to film as a teaching and research tool. The trend during the past half-decade has been impressive. A burgeoning number of courses based on film appears in college catalogs; nearly every historical gathering, be it the annual AHA conventions or more regional and specialized ones, includes at least one session involving the film (and they are among the best attended sessions); a journal on the subject, *Film & History,* appears quarterly; the *AHA Newsletter* now publishes a section entitled "Media and History"; and a few dissertations soon will assume filmic form. Seemingly it is no longer necessary to convince the profession of the worth of the celluloid source for history.

A difficult task challenges those historians converted to film. They must devise proper methodologies for their use of the film and conceptualize the relationships of film and history. Scant work has been done in either direction. The following bibliofilmography provides a base upon which to begin to construct the theories and methodologies the historians will need if they are to make fullest use of film. Unfortunately, the reading of any or all of the essays or books or the viewing of the films listed below will not guarantee a harvest of philosophical insight into the film, but perhaps coupled with the increasing practical experience historians are getting with films these will plant the seeds from which such insights eventually will grow.

The essays and books suggested below vary considerably. Whenever possible, the bibliography eschews the practical for the more theoretical. Some of the materials will link the historian with film as either a teaching device or research source; others will reveal in film certain characteristics to which historians can relate their traditional methodologies; not a few treat the filmmakers' concern with neorealism; still others attempt to explain what film is and what it can accomplish, information vital to historians who want to master the use of the film. Not lacking in this bibliography is the call to the historian to become a filmmaker. Perhaps of all the materials suggested below, the essays of Joan Mellen and Eugene C. McCreary, contained in Chapter 2 above, offer the best conceptual base upon which historians can build.

Written Sources

Arbaugh, Dorothy. "Motion Pictures and the Future Historian," *American Archivist,* Vol. II (April, 1939), pp. 106-114.
> A history of the foundation (1935) and early years of the Division of Motion Pictures and Sound Recordings of the National Archives which still serves as a practical guide to the goals and work of that Division. It accentuates the importance of film to the historian.

Armes, Roy. *Film and Reality: An Historical Survey* (Baltimore: Penguin, 1974).
> An important introduction to the study of film. Although only one part deals specifically with the title of this book, linking film with reality, the other two parts on illusion and modernism are sufficiently interesting and informative to make their reading worthwhile.

Arrowsmith, William. "Film as Educator," *Journal of Aesthetic Education,* Vol. III, No. 3 (July, 1969), pp. 75-83.
> One of the most powerful and pursuasive statements on the importance of the film to students and teachers. "In humanistic education the future lies with film."

Bachmann, Gideon. "Reappraisals: A Novel Look at Some Uses of the Cinematic Past, and a Report on the Newsreel Film Festival in Grado, Italy," *Film Quarterly,* Vol. XXVI, No. 2 (Winter, 1972-1973), pp. 10-14.
> The use of the newsreel to get "varied" views of the past.

Bachmann, Gideon, Robert Drew, Richard Leacock, and D. A. Pennebaker. "The Frontiers of Realist Cinema," in Richard Dyer MacCann (ed.), *Film: A Montage of Theories* (New York: Dutton, 1966), pp. 289-300.

 Questions of how the camera can catch "the truth," objectivity in filmmaking, and what reality is concern these practitioners of the new "direct cinema."

Barsam, Richard Meran. *Nonfiction Film: A Critical History* (New York: Dutton, 1973).

 Illustration of one approach to the criticism and discussion of film. Mainly descriptive and qualitative, the criticism lacks a conceptual framework for the study and use of documentaries. Yet it provides a solid base for those beginning to study and work with documentaries. It presents in orderly and clear fashion a history of the major movements, filmmakers, and films.

Burns, E. Bradford. "The Latin American Film, Realism, and the Historian," *History Teacher,* Vol. VI, No. 4 (August, 1973), pp. 569-574.

 Young Latin American filmmakers concerned with recreating and reinterpreting on film the histories of their nations. They are using many of the methods of the historian and ably applying them to their filmic studies.

Cavel, Stanley. *The World Viewed: Reflections on the Ontology of Film* (New York: Viking, 1971).

 The author treats the fundamental question of what film is.

Collier, Jr., John. *Visual Anthropology: Photography as a Research Method* (New York: Holt, Rinehart and Winston, 1967).

 A meaty and indispensable study for the social scientist interested in using the photograph or film for research and study.

Film and the Historian (London: British University Film Council, 1969).

 A combined reprint of *University Vision,* No. 1 (February, 1968) and the monograph *Film and the Historian,* an edited transcript of the conference held at University College, London, April, 1968. These essays and discussions are fundamental.

French, Warren. "An 'Eye' for America," in Marshall W. Fishwick (ed.), *American Studies in Transition* (Philadelphia: University of Pennsylvania Press, 1964), pp. 36-52.
   Smoothly written essay advocating the need to develop the senses along with the intellect. It is not enough to read about the past; the scholar and student must develop an "eye" for it as well. The essay concludes with a discussion of the benefits of studying films.

Grenville, J. A. S. *Film as History: The Nature of Film Evidence* (Birmingham, England: University of Birmingham, 1971).
   Contains the basic information on the use the historian can make of film but is devoid of any insights into conceptualization or methodology. Unfortunately, the essay is not as attractive as the title.

Grierson, John. "First Principles of Documentary," in Forsyth Hardy (ed.), *Grierson on Documentary* (New York: Praeger, 1971), pp.145-156.
   Some of the master's basic ideas on the importance and purpose of the documentary.

Griffin, Patrick. "Film, Document, and the Historian," *Film & History,* Vol. II, No. 2 (May, 1972), pp. 1-6.
   Some practical statements on the historian's use of the film as a document.

―――. "The Making of Goodbye Billy," *Film & History,* Vol. II, No. 2 (May, 1972), pp. 6-9.
   A historian who has made a historical documentary discusses the process and problems.

Hoffmann, Stanley. "Introduction" in *The Sorrow and the Pity: A Film by Marcel Ophuls* (New York: Outerbridge & Lazard, 1972), pp. vii-xxvi.
   Critical remarks revealing the strengths and weaknesses of the documentary.

Houston, Penelope. "The Nature of Evidence," *Sight and Sound,* Vol. 36, No. 2 (1967), pp. 88-92.

> A very perceptive essay that recognizes the difficulty of using film as historical evidence and yet understands that it is an invaluable source to understand the past. In the view of traditional historical methodology, the film is considered to have many weaknesses, but, as the author aptly observes, "It is perhaps unreasonable for historians to criticise film men for not doing their own job for them." Film as evidence, the author concludes, is "untrustworthy, superficial, vulnerable to every kind of distortion; and at the same time irreplaceable, necessary, a source material that no twentieth century historian ought to disregard."

Hughes, William. "Proposal for a Course on Films and History," *University Vision* (London), No. 8 (January, 1972), pp. 9-18.

> Unique essay suggesting what the historian needs to know about film as well as what he can read and see to acquire that knowledge. In short, it outlines an interesting training program.

Jackson, Martin A. "Film as a Source Material: Some Preliminary Notes toward a Methodology," *Journal of Inter-Disciplinary History,* Vol. IV, No. 1 (Summer, 1973), pp. 73-80.

> Outlines successfully some of the problems and rewards of film research but does not come to grips with the elusive goal of suggesting "guideposts along the road to a useful research methodology."

Kouwenhoven, John A. "American Studies: Words or Things?" in Marshall W. Fishwick (ed.), *American Studies in Transition* (Philadelphia: University of Pennsylvania Press, 1964), pp. 15-35.

> An excellent statement on the growing move away from reliance upon verbal evidence in cultural analysis.

Landesman, Rocco. "The Celluloid Intellectual," *Yale/Theater,* Vol. III, No. 1 (Fall, 1970), pp. 2-14.

> A witty view of the intellectual's attraction to the cinema.

Loy, Jane M. "Latin America through Film: Problems and Possibilities," in *Proceedings of the Pacific Coast Council on Latin American Studies,* Vol. II (1973), pp. 39-52.
  A lucid discussion of the problems of using film in the classroom which also indicates the advantages of giving visual contact with the subject. The film successfully recreates a sense of the past, as well as reflects the attitudes of filmmakers and their society.

Marcorelles, Louis. *Living Cinema: New Directions in Contemporary Filmmaking* (New York: Praeger, 1973).
  Realism in cinema discussed under the title of "direct cinema." It offers a basic history of it from the Italians through the most recent Third World group. It provides an excellent background for a knowledge of the aims of filmic realism.

McCreary, Eugene C. "Film and History: Some Thoughts on Their Interrelationship," *Societas,* II (Winter, 1971), pp. 51-66.
  Reprinted in its entirety in Chapter 2 above.

Mellen, Joan. "Film and Style: The Fictional Documentary," *Antioch Review,* Vol. 32, No. 3 (1973), pp. 403-425.
  Reprinted in its entirety in Chapter 2 above.

Metz, Christian. *Film Language: A Semiotics of the Cinema* (New York: Oxford University Press, 1974).
  Some philosophical discussions of the components of film language, the concept of reality, and aesthetic theory.

Murphy, William T. "Film at the National Archives: A Reference Article," *Film & History,* Vol. III, No. 3 (September, 1972), pp. 7-13.
  A practical guide indicating in very general terms the kinds of film collections held by the National Archives.

———. "The National Archives and the Historian's Use of Film," *History Teacher,* Vol. VI, No. 1 (November, 1972), pp. 119-134.
  Highly informative article explaining how the National Archives can help the historian interested in film and also discusses the use historians can make of films.

O'Connor, John E. "Historians and Film: Some Problems and Prospects," *History Teacher,* Vol. VI, No. 4 (August, 1973), pp. 543-552.
    A report indicating the increasing use of film by historians.

Perkins, V. F. *Film as Film: Understanding and Judging Movies* (Baltimore: Penguin, 1972).
    A helpful guide to formulating film criticism.

Peterson, Arthur. "History at the Cinema: A Guide for the Movie-Going History Student," *History Teacher,* Vol. VII, No. 1 (November, 1973), pp. 79-88.
    State of Siege as a case study for using the historical, fictional documentary as a source for the study of history. The author provides useful information on the film and correlates the actual events with the filmic version.

Pronay, Nicholas, Betty R. Smith, and Tom Hastie. *The Use of Film in History Teaching* (London: The Historical Association, 1972).
    A short, basic, useful guide.

Raack, R. C. "Clio's Dark Mirror: The Documentary Film in History," *History Teacher,* Vol. VI, No. 1 (November, 1972), pp. 109-118.
    Essentially a plea for historians to make history films.

Roads, Christopher M. "Film as Historical Evidence," *Journal of the Society of Archivists* (London), Vol. III, No. 4 (October, 1966), pp. 183-191.
    An excellent introduction to the difficulties historians will have in using film as a source. It also makes some valuable observations on the film as a source.

Roemer, Michael. "The Surfaces of Reality," in Richard Dyer MacCann (ed.), *Film: A Montage of Theories* (New York: Dutton, 1966), pp. 255-268.
    Film carefully planned can give the effect of reality.

Rossellini, Roberto. *Diálogos Casi Socráticos con Roberto Rossellini* (Barcelona: Editorial Anagrama, 1972).
    Expression of Rossellini's philosophy concerning history on film, some ideas on neorealism, and the main themes film should be concerned with.

Rotha, Paul. "Some Principles of Documentary," in Daniel Talbot (ed.), *Film: An Anthology* (Berkeley and Los Angeles: University of California Press, 1970), pp. 234-246.
    An excellent essay with many insights into the importance of the documentary.

———. "A Panorama of History," *Screen* (London), Vol. 14, No. 4 (Winter, 1973-1974), pp. 83-111.
    One of the most important directors of neorealistic films speaks on the connection of film and history in his own work.

Samuels, Stuart, and Robert Rosen. "Film and the Historian," *AHA Newsletter,* Vol. II, No. 2 (May, 1973), pp. 31-37.
    The authors hold that the historian can make three principal uses of film: visual aid, historical evidence, and as social and intellectual history. They tell how they use film in a course entitled "The Film as Social and Intellectual History."

Tudor, Andrew. "The Many Mythologies of Realism," *Screen* (London), Vol. 13, No. 1 (Spring, 1972), pp. 27-35.
    Important essay to understand the search for realism in films. The author concludes that there is no "absolute aesthetic standard" for realism and leaves for further thought the assertion, "... what is important is not what can be claimed as a realistic representation, but what *appears* as real: plausibility."

———. *Theories of Film* (London: Secker and Warburg, 1974).
    Short book introducing some of the major approaches to the study of film with emphasis on the aesthetics of realism.

Vanderwood, Paul J. "Hollywood and History: Does Film Make the Connection?" *Proceedings of the Pacific Coast Council on Latin American Studies,* Vol. II (1973), pp. 53-59.
    Cautioning that film may be the most difficult document for a historian to analyze, the author suggests four ways for historians to study and use the film: "(1) as a document that reflects the times in which it was produced (a primary document); (2) as a pictorial representation of 'the way things were or happened' (a primary document); as the recreation of historical events (a secondary document); (4) as

a springboard to present and discuss historical events, trends and ideas (a teaching tool)."

Young, Colin, "Film and Social Change," *Journal of Aesthetic Education,* Vol. III, No. 3 (July, 1969), pp. 21-27.
　　Among other things, this disjointed essay reveals the growing affinity between fictional and nonfictional documentaries.

Zavattini, Cesare. "Some Ideas on the Cinema," in Richard Dyer MacCann (ed.), *Film: A Montage of Theories* (New York: Dutton, 1966), pp. 216-228.
　　One of the chief exponents of neorealism asserts that the duty of film is to reflect reality and impel the viewer to confront it.

Filmic Sources

Making of a Documentary. University of California Extension Media Center.
　　A 22-minute film explaining many of the problems of producing a TV news documentary, focusing on the ethical and practical difficulties of editing. The similarities of method with the historian's traditional methodologies are striking.

Mini Course on Film Study. Contemporary Films/McGraw-Hill (Hightstown, N.Y./Evanston, Ill./San Francisco).
　　Approximately six hours of viewing time. Live action and animation, document and dream, slow motion and fantasy, and quick-cutting collage, these are only a few of the possible permutations of the film experience. The films incorporate all the basic elements of visual communication and can readily instruct the viewer in the language of films. The mini course is divided into the following subjects: the creative use of actuality, the varieties of film experience, the narrative and film, and the language of images.

Neorealism. University of California Extension Media Center.
　　A 30-minute film examining the neorealist movement in Italian filmmaking with appropriate clips and interviews.

Satyajit Ray. University of California Extension Media Center.
A 28-minute study of the Indian filmmaker, exploring his films, views, and methods. Ray is primarily concerned with a realistic depiction of Indian society. He often takes as a theme the conflict of tradition and modernity.

Bibliography of Latin American Cinema

The rich and varied Latin American cinema merits more attention than it has received. Amazingly little has been written about it – in any language. Articles on the subject far outnumber the books, of which there are hardly any other than in Spanish and Portuguese. And even in those two major languages of Latin America the bibliography is lean.

Until Michael Myerson edited his miscellaneous assortment of screenplays and comments, *Memories of Underdevelopment: The Revolutionary Films of Cuba,* in 1973, there was not a single book about Latin America films in English. Most film journals ignore that area. The notable exception is *Cinéaste* (New York), whose pages regularly provide the best and most complete information on the subject in English. Since 1967, it consistently has published insightful essays and interviews on the Latin American cinema.

In recent years the French have evinced a growing enthusiasm for the films of the young Latin Americans. *La Revue du Cinéma Image et Son* (Paris), in particular, has carried some perceptive essays on the Latin American cinema, interviews with some of the leading directors, and reviews of their best films. The new Chilean cinema attracted considerable attention in France, and, to a lesser degree, so did Brazil's Cinema Nôvo and Cuban films.

In Spanish, the most complete coverage of Latin American cinema appears in *Cine Cubano* published in Havana. The essays and interviews in that illustrated, imaginative journal are always meaty and informative. *Hablemos del Cine* (Lima) and the short-lived *Primer Plano* (Valparaiso) are its only real competitors and neither has had the coverage, experience, and circulation of the highly influential Cuban journal. The Cinemateca of the

University of Mexico publishes a small but rewarding film journal, *Cinemateca,* whose first issue came out in 1971 and whose fourth bears the date December, 1973. Those four issues contain considerable information on the "cinemateca" movement in Latin America as well as some thoughtful essays on films of social concern being made throughout the region. It ranks as the best film magazine published in Mexico and has the potential of becoming one of the leading Latin American journals on the cinema.

In Portuguese, the major film journal is *Filme Cultura,* published in Rio de Janeiro since 1966. It focuses on Brazilian film topics and personalities but also reports on important international cinematic news and events. Nearly every issue includes interviews; other articles analyze the technical, artistic, or educational aspects of Brazilian films.

The following bibliography on the Latin American cinema is by no means complete. The emphasis falls on the "new" cinema which has developed in the past two decades and variously termed "direct," "revolutionary," or "militant." (In Brazil it bore the distinctive title of "Cinema Nôvo.") The common characteristic of this new cinema has been its concern with Latin American reality. This bibliography serves primarily as an introduction to the highly important but sadly neglected Latin American cinema of social realism. Hopefully the works cited will provide basic information for further studies. Much remains to be done.

Achugar, Walter. "Walter Achugar on Latin American Cinema," *Cinéaste,* Vol. IV, No. 3 (Winter, 1970-1971), pp. 35, 52.

Ackermann, Jean Marie. *Films of a Changing World: A Critical International Guide* (Washington, D.C.: Society for International Development, 1972).

A mixture of reviews and commentaries first published in the *International Development Review.* Scattered at random throughout are reviews of films from and about Latin America. Useful index guides the reader.

Alemán, Mario Rodríguez. "Bosquejo Histórico del Cine Cubano," *Cine Cubano,* Nos. 23/24/25, pp. 25-35.

Alfaro, Hugo. "Diez Años de Cine Cubano," *Cine & Medios* (Buenos Aires), Año I, No. 2 (Spring, 1969), pp. 14-17.

Alvarez, Isabelle. "Revolution versus Entertainment: What Directions for the Film Medium?" *Atlas,* October, 1971, pp. 57-59.
: The author distinguishes between the so-called "leftist" European cinema and the true militancy of committed Third World movie makers, particularly those of Latin America.

Alvarez, Carlos. "Una Historia que Está Comenzando: Colombia," *Cine Cubano,* Nos. 63/64/65, pp. 41-50.
: A brief history of Colombian film with emphasis on the decade of the 1960s.

Alvarez, Santiago. "Conversación con Santiago Alvarez," *Cine Cubano,* Nos. 78/79/80, pp. 80-91.

Andrade, Joaquim Pedro de. "Joaquim Pedro de Andrade por él Mismo," *Cine & Medios* (Buenos Aires), Año II, No. 5, pp. 21-25.

Arai, Alberto T. *Voluntad Cinematográfica: Ensayo para una Estética del Cine* (Mexico: Editorial Cultura, 1937).
: An early essay that foresaw the potential for film as an expression of national culture in Latin America.

"Argentine Censorship. Protest Films . . . But for Export Only," *Atlas,* October, 1971, pp. 56-57.
: Short interviews with Mario Sábato and Raimundo Gleyzer.

Balde, Gibril. "Blood of the Condor," *Cinéaste,* Vol. IV, No. 3 (Winter, 1970-1971), p. 11.

Belmans, Jacques. "Critique et Realite Sociales dans le Cinema Novo," *Études Cinématographiques,* Nos. 93-96 (Paris: Lettres Modernes, 1972), pp. 41-60.

Bernardet, Jean-Claude. "Para um Cinema Dinámico," *Revista Civilização Brasileira* (Rio de Janeiro), No. 2 (May, 1965), pp. 219-226.

Birri, Fernando. "Cinema et Sous-Developpement," *Cine Cubano,* Nos. 42/43/44, pp. 13-21.

Blanco, Jorge Ayala. *La Aventura del Cine Mexicano* (Mexico: Ediciones Era, 1968).
: Splendid study of Mexican films concentrating on the period from 1930 onward. With much sociological insight, Blanco

treats his broad subject by themes (the Revolution, the city, the province, violence, the family and others). His appendix of "fundamental films" made in Mexico is very useful. This book is well written, highly informative, and very sophisticated in its approach to film. It ranks as a basic work for insight into the Mexican cinema.

Chili: Le Cinema de L'Unité Populaire," *Ecran* (Paris), No. 22 (February, 1974), pp. 13-20.

An introduction to the Chilean cinema, 1970-1973, followed by interviews with Patricio Guzman, Miguel Littin, Raul Ruiz, and Helvio Soto.

Colina, Enrique, and Daniel D. Torres. "Ideologia del Melodrama en el Viejo Cine Latinoamericano," *Cine Cubano,* Nos. 73/74/75, pp. 27-39.

Excellent essay documenting the elitist attitudes and stereotypes dominating the traditional Latin American film industry.

Collazos, Oscar. "Cine Colombiano: Por Quién, Para Quién, Contra Quienes?" *Cine Cubano,* Nos. 76/77, pp. 34-39.

Coo, Carlos Ossa. *Historia del Cine Chileno* (Santiago: Quimantu, 1971).

Crowdua, Gary. "The Spring 1972 Cuban Film Festival Bust," *Film Society Review,* Vol. 7, Nos. 7-9 (March, April, May, 1972), pp. 23-36.

Dahl, Gustavo. "Cinema Nôvo e seu Público," *Revista Civilizacão Brasileira,* Nos. 11-12 (December, 1966-March, 1967), pp. 192-202.

Dahl, Gustavo, Carlos Diegues, David Neves, Paulo César Saraceni, and Alex Viany. "Vitória do Cinema Nôvo," *Revista Civilização Brasileira,* No. 2 (May, 1965), pp. 227-248.

Ehrmann, Hans. "Cine Chileno: Experanzas . . . Otra Vez," *La Quinta Rueda* (Santiago), April, 1973, pp. 10-11.

Espinosa, Julio García. "Nuestro Cine Documental," *Cine Cubano,* Nos. 23/24/25, pp. 3-21.

History of the documentary film making of the Cuban Film Institute, 1959-1963.

——. "For an Imperfect Cinema," *Afterimage* (London), No. 3 (Summer, 1971), pp. 54-67. For the Spanish-language version see *Cine Cubano,* Nos. 66/67, pp. 46-53.

Fisher, Jack. "Politics by Magic: Antonio das Mortes," *The Film Journal,* Vol. I, No. 1 (Spring, 1971), pp. 32-38.

Francia, Aldo. "Cine y Revolución," *Primer Plano* (Valparaiso), Vol. II, No. 5 (Summer, 1973), pp. 69-76.

——. " 'Todo Cine Es Un Engaño.' Entrevista a Aldo Francia," *Primer Plano* (Valparaiso), Vol. I, No. 3 (Winter, 1972), pp. 3-17.

Galindo, Alejandro. *Una Radiografia Histórica del Cine Mexicano* (Mexico: Fondo de Cultura Popular, 1968).
This Mexican director understands the potential of film to complement national culture and frankly admits that the Mexican film industry presents a false image of Mexican culture.

Gardies, Rene. "Les Films de Glauber Rocha: Presentation d'une Méthode," *La Revue du Cinéma Image et Son,* No. 271 (April, 1973), pp. 66-91.

——. *Glauber Rocha* (Paris: Editions Seghers, 1974).

Gautier, Guy. "Chili: La Premiere Annee," *La Revue du Cinéma Image et Son,* No. 270 (March, 1973), pp. 1-22.

Getino, Octavio. "Algunas Preguntas a Octavio Getino," *Cine Cubano,* Nos. 73/74/75, pp. 72-79.

Getino, Octavio, and Fernando Solanas. "Apuntes para un Juicio Crítico Descolonizado," *Cine del Tercer Mundo* (Montevideo), No. 2 (November, 1970), pp. 75-101.
Elaborating on the idea of what constitutes the "cinema of liberation," this excellent essay provides a critical basis from which to judge the new Latin American cinema.

Gili, Jean A. "Fantastique, Magie et Réalité dans L'Oeuvre de Ruy Guerra," *Études Cinématographiques,* Nos. 93-96 (Paris: Lettres Modernes, 1972), pp. 124-138.

Gómez, Manuel Octavio. "Entrevista con Manuel Octavio Gómez," *Cine Cubano,* Nos. 71/72, pp. 32-36.

Gomezjara, Francisco A., and Delia Selene de Dios. *Sociologia del Cine* (Mexico: Sep/Setentas, 1973).
   A useful discussion of the cinema as a social force. It contains some valuable statistics as well.

Gonzaga, Adhemar, and P. E. Salles. *70 Anos de Cinema Brasileiro* (Rio de Janeiro: Editora Expressão e Cultura, 1966).

Grelier, Robert. "Brésil: Entretiens avec José Carlos Avellar, Sérgio Muniz, Geraldo Sarno," *La Revue du Cinéma Image et Son*, No. 270 (March, 1973), pp. 24-36.

Grinberg, Miguel. "Las Olas Bajan Turbias: El Viejo 'Nuevo Cine' Argentino," *Cine & Medios* (Buenos Aires), Vol. I, No. 2 (Spring, 1969), pp. 34-40.

Guerra, Ruy. "Entretien avec Ruy Guerra," *Études Cinématographiques*, Nos. 93-96 (Paris: Lettres Modernes, 1972), pp. 80-123.

Guzmán, Patricio. " 'Mas Vale una Sólida Formación Política que la Destreza Artesanal': Entrevista a Patricio Guzman," *Primer Plano* (Valparaiso), Vol. II, No. 5 (Summer, 1973), pp. 19-36.

Hijar, Alberto. *Hacia Un Tercer Cine* (Mexico: Un. Autónoma de Méjico, 1972).

Hitchens, Gordon. "The Way To Make a Future: A Conversation with Glauber Rocha," *Film Quarterly*, Fall, 1970, pp. 27-30.

Irigoyen, Oribe. *Cine. Crítica. Espectador* (Montevideo: Pueblos Unidos, 1972).
   Although a general survey of the cinema, the emphasis falls on what has been happening in Latin America and films of social realism. There is a section on the Uruguayan cinema.

Kavanagh, Thomas M. "Imperialism and the Revolutionary Cinema: Glauber Rocha's *Antonio-das-Mortes*," *Journal of Modern Literature*, Vol. III, No. 2 (April, 1973), pp. 201-213.
   An excellent and meaty discussion of Rocha's film.

Lajous-Vargas, Adrián. "Mexico, the Frozen Revolution," *Cinéaste*, Vol. IV, No. 3 (Winter, 1970-1971), pp. 36-37.

Littin, Miguel. "Apuntes de Filmación," *La Quinta Rueda* (Santiago), November, 1972, p. 13.

——. *El Chacal de Nahueltoro* (Santiago: Editorial Zig-Zag, 1970).
   A long and fascinating discussion of the film between Littin and those who cooperated with him (pp. 7-91) precedes the screenplay.

——. "Film in Chile: An Interview with Miguel Littin," *Cinéaste*, Vol. IV, No. 4 (Spring, 1971), pp. 4-17.

——. "Nuevo Cine, Nuevos Realizadores, Nuevos Filmes: Entrevista a Miguel Littin," *Cine Cubano*, Nos. 63/64/65, pp. 1-6.

——. " 'Primero Hay que Aprovechar el Dividendo Ideológico del Cine': Entrevista a Miguel Littin," *Primer Plano* (Valparaiso), Vol. I, No. 2 (Fall, 1972), pp. 4-16.

——. "La Tierra Prometida," *Crisis* (Buenos Aires), No. 2 (June, 1973), pp. 38-42.
   Littin summarizes the story of the historically based film *The Promised Land;* it concerns a 1934 rural uprising in Chile.

Loy, Jane M. "Classroom Films on Latin America: A Review of the Present Situation with Some Suggestions for the Future," *The History Teacher*, Vol. VII, No. 1 (November, 1973), pp. 89-98.

——. *Latin America: Sights and Sounds. A Guide to Motion Pictures and Music for College Courses* (Gainesville, Fla.: Consortium of Latin American Studies Programs, 1973).
   After a brief introduction acknowledging the importance of film in the classroom, this guide recommends and rates a large number of films. It contains helpful information on content, rental rates, and distributors.

MacBean, James Roy. "La Hora de los Hornos," *Film Quarterly*, Fall, 1970, pp. 31-37.

Mahieu, José Agustín. *Breve Historia del Cine Argentino* (Buenos Aires: Editorial Universitaria de Buenos Aires, 1966).

Martínez, Tomás Eloy. *La Obra de Ayala y Torre Nilson en las Estructuras del Cine Argentino* (Buenos Aires: Ediciones Culturales Argentinas, 1961).

Martins, Luciano. "Terra em Transe," *Revista Civilização Brasileira*, No. 14 (July, 1967), pp. 227-232.

Matas, Julio. "Theater and Cinematography," in Carmelo Mesa-Lago (ed.), *Revolutionary Change in Cuba: Polity, Economy, Society* (Pittsburgh: University of Pittsburgh Press, 1971), pp. 436-442.
    A very brief history of the Cuban cinema.

Miller, Clyde. "Filmmakers of Churubusco," *Américas*, Vol. 26, No. 4 (April, 1974), pp. 15-20.
    An indication of the woes that have beset the Mexican film industry since 1946. The acquisition of equipment and facilities seems to have replaced a search for quality.

Moral G., Fernando del. "Contra el Cine Comercial Latinoamericano," *Novedades* (Mexico City), September 15, 1974, Magazine Section *La Onda*, pp. 2-3, 12.
    A summary of the proceedings at the conference "El Cine Latinoamericano" held at the Centro Universitario de Estudios Cinematográficos, University of Mexico, August 12-25, 1974.

Munizaga, Giselle. "Algunas Ideas sobre lo Ideológico en el Cine," *Revista EAC* (Catholic University of Chile), No. 2 (1972), pp. 58-61.
    The title suggests much, but the essay covers little more than the idea that the cinema defines social behavior.

Murat, Ulyses Petit de. *Este Cine Argentino* (Buenos Aires: Ediciones del Cano de Tespis, 1959).
    An essay on the development of the Argentine film industry.

Myerson, Michael (ed.). *Memories of Underdevelopment: The Revolutionary Films of Cuba* (New York: Grossman Publishers, 1973).
    An introduction sets the new Cuban film industry into its revolutionary perspective. Then follow the screen scripts of *Memories of Underdevelopment* and Part III of *Lucia*. The collection closes with information on other Cuban films, features and documentaries, as well as on film poster art.

Neves, David E. *Cinema Nôvo no Brasil* (Petrópolis: Vozes, 1966).
A brief, weak introduction to Cinema Nôvo. Chapter VI contains biographical information on filmmakers associated with the movement.

Nicholson, Irene. "Mexican Films: Their Past and Their Future," *The Quarterly of Film, Radio, and Television,* Vol. 10, No. 3 (Spring, 1956), pp. 248-249.

Olivova, Drahomira. "A Crítica e o Nôvo Cinema," *Revista Civilização Brasileira,* Nos. 9 and 10 (September-November, 1966), pp. 205-216.

Piazza, Luis Guillermo. "A Propósito de la Cineteca," *Novedades* (Mexico), September 15, 1974, Magazine Section *La Onda,* p. 5.
Taking to task — very sarcastically — the new trends in Latin American cinema, this instructive piece of criticism represents very well the "colonial" mentality characteristic of the traditional Latin American cinema.

Pick, Zuzana Myriam. "Le Cinema Chilien sous le Signe de L'Union Populaire (1970-1973)," *Positif,* No. 155 (January, 1974), pp. 35-41.
An excellent introduction to the Chilean Cinema followed by a chronology of films produced in Chile, 1968-1972, and a bio-filmography.

Prédal, René. "Une Tradition Populaire Vivante ou L'Esthétique de la Révolte," *Études Cinématographiques,* Nos. 93-96 (Paris: Lettres Modernes, 1972), pp. 5-40.
An informative study of Brazil's Cinema Nôvo.

Quesada, Luis. "Brazil's Film-Makers Move to the City: The Force of Realism," *Atlas,* September, 1971, pp. 51-52.
A review of Carlos Diegues's *A Cidade Grande* which puts the film into perspective: the conflict between the past and present.

Racz, Juan-Andrés. "El Chacal de Nahueltoro," *Cinéaste,* Vol. IV, No. 3 (Winter, 1970-1971), pp. 37-38.

Reyes, Aurelio de los. "Hacia un cine mexicano," *Revista de la Universidad de México* (Mexico City), Vol. XXVIII, No. 3 (November, 1973), pp. 25-28.

The author documents the fact that the first Mexican films, until 1917, were dedicated to "reality."

Riera, Emilio Garcia. *Historia Documental del Cine Mexicano,* 4 vols. (Mexico: Ediciones Era, 1969-1972).
Covers the years 1926-1951.

Rocha, Glauber. "Cabezas Cortadas: Interview with Glauber Rocha," *Afterimage,* No. 3 (Summer, 1971), pp. 68-77.

———. "Carta de Glauber Rocha," *Cine Cubano,* Nos. 71/72, pp. 1-11.

———. "Cinema Nôvo vs. Cultural Colonialism: An Interview with Glauber Rocha," *Cinéaste,* Vol. IV, No. 1 (Summer, 1970), pp. 2-9.

———. *Deus e o Diablo na Terra do Sol* (Rio de Janeiro: Editora Civilização Brasileira, 1965).
Essays by Rocha and others on the significance of this important film in addition to the screenplay.

———. "Uma Estética da Fome," *Revista Civilização Brasileira,* No. 3 (July, 1965), pp. 165-170.

———. *Revisión Crítica del Cine Brasileño* (Madrid: Editorial Fundamentos, 1971). The Portuguese-language edition is *Revisão Crítica do Cinema Brasileiro* (Rio de Janeiro: Editora Civilização Brasileira, 1963).
A digest of Rocha's ideas on film.

———. "Somos los Heraldos de la Revolución: Entrevista con Glauber Rocha," *Cine Cubano,* Nos. 73/74/75, pp. 40-46.

———. " 'We Are the Harbingers of Revolution': An Interview with Glauber Rocha," *Atlas,* October, 1971, pp. 54-55.

Rocha, Glauber, and Augusto M. Torres. *Glauber Rocha y Cabezas Cortadas* (Barcelona: Editorial Anagrama, 1970).
A catchall of considerable interest. In the first part Rocha discusses his films; the second part is his screenplay *Cabezas Cortadas.*

Ruiz, Raúl. " 'Prefiero Registrar antes que Mistificar el Proceso Chileno': Entrevista a Raul Ruiz," *Primer Plano* (Valparaiso), Vol. I, No. 4 (Spring, 1972), pp. 3-21.

Sanjines, Jorge. "Un Cine Militante," *Cine Cubano*, No. 68, pp. 45-47.

———. "Cine Revolucionario: La Experiencia Boliviana," *Cine Cubano*, Nos. 76/77, pp. 1-15.

———. "Cinema and Revolution," *Cinéaste*, Vol. IV, No. 3 (Winter, 1970-1971), pp. 13-14.

———. "Conversación con un Cineasta Revolucionario: Jorge Sanjines," *Cine Cubano*, Nos. 73/74/75, pp. 1-7.

———. "El Coraje del Pueblo: Nuevo Filme de Jorge Sanjines," *Cine Cubano*, Nos. 71/72, pp. 46-51.

———. "The Courage of the People: An Interview with Jorge Sanjines," *Cinéaste*, Vol. V, No. 2 (Spring, 1972), pp. 18-20.

———. "Jorge Sanjines: Una Entrevista," *Cine Cubano*, Nos. 71/72, pp. 52-59.

———. "Sobre Ukamau," *Cine Cubano*, No. 48, pp. 28-33.

———. "A Talk with Jorge Sanjines," *Cinéaste*, Vol. IV, No. 3 (Winter, 1970-1971), p. 12.

———. "Ukamau and Yawar Mallku: An Interview with Jorge Sanjines," *Afterimage*, No. 3 (Summer, 1971), pp. 40-53.

Santos, Nélson Pereira dos. "Entretien avec Nélson Pereira dos Santos," *Études Cinématographiques*, Nos. 93-96 (Paris: Lettres Modernes, 1972), pp. 61-74.

Sauvage, Pierre. "Cine Cubano," *Film Comment*, Vol. 8, No. 1 (Spring, 1972), pp. 24-31.

Schwarz, Roberto. "O Cinema e os Fuzis," *Revista Civilização Brasileira*, Nos. 9 and 10 (November, 1966), pp. 217-222.

Sheldin, Michael. "Case Study vs. Process Study: Two Films Made for Italian Television," *Film Quarterly*, Vol. 27, No. 3 (Spring, 1974), pp. 27-39.

> The author compares *The Night of San Juan* (most often referred to as *The Courage of the People*) by Jorge Sanjines with the Italian film *San Michele Had a Rooster*. The author sees the Sanjines film as one made with and for the masses, dealing concretely with the workers' day-to-day experience and the means of throwing off oppression.

Silva, Alberto. "O Filme de Cangaço," *Filme Cultura* (Rio de Janeiro), Vol. II, No. 17 (November-December, 1970), pp. 42-49.

> A brief history of the "bandit" film in Brazil with some indication of the social significance of the genre.

Solanas, Fernando. "Cinema as a Gun: An Interview with Fernando Solanas," *Cinéaste,* Vol. III, No. 2 (Fall, 1969), pp. 18-26.

> The interview gives some insight into the ideology of one of the foremost makers of "revolutionary cinema" as well as provides some valuable information on the film *The Hour of the Furnaces.*

———. "Fernando Solanas: An Interview," *Film Quarterly,* Vol. 24, No. 1 (Fall, 1970), pp. 37-43.

Solanas, Fernando, and Octavio Getino. *Cine, Cultura y Descolonización* (Buenos Aires: Siglo Veintiuno, 1973).

> An anthology of the writings and pronouncements of two articulate Argentine filmmakers. Their ideas are essential to understand Latin America's new "revolutionary cinema."

———. "Toward a Third Cinema," *Cinéaste,* Vol. IV, No. 3 (Winter, 1970-1971), pp. 1-14.

Soto, Helvio. "Entretien avec Helvio Soto," *Cinéma 72,* No. 164 (1972), pp. 76-85.

———. " 'Para Ser un Cineaste Revolucionario Primero Hay que Ser un Buen Cineasta': Entrevista a Helvio Soto," *Primer Plano* (Valparaiso), No. 1 (Summer, 1972), pp. 4-26.

Teixeira, Jaime Rodrigues, Octavio Ianni, and Antonio Lima. "O Desafio do Cinema Nôvo," *Revista Civilização Brasileira,* No. 8 (July, 1966), pp. 227-242.

Tessier, Max. "Note sur *Os Herdeiros (Les Héritiers):* Un Révélateur du Brésil," *Études Cinématographiques,* Nos. 93-96 (Paris: Lettres Modernes, 1972), pp. 75-79.

Torres, Augusto M., and Manuel Perez Estremera. "Chile: Introduction to Chilean Cinema," *CTVD: Cinema-TV-Digest,* No. 33 (Fall, 1972), pp. 31-32.

———. *Nuevo Cine Latinoamericano* (Barcelona: Editorial Anagrama, 1973).

 This book is divided into chapters by country and provides basic information on some of the recent film activities in Argentina, Bolivia, Brazil, Chile, Colombia, Cuba, Mexico, Peru, Uruguay, and Venezuela. The emphasis falls on films of sociological and political importance. Although there is much useful information, there is also evidence of some errors. This book is a handy guide to the "new" film movements in much of Latin America.

Urteaga, Enrique. " 'Operación Alfa': Clarificando con Rabia. Entrevista a Enrique Urteaga," *Primer Plano* (Valparaiso), Vol. II, No. 5 (Summer, 1973), pp. 3-18.

Vega, Pastor. "Cuba: El Cine, La Cultura Nacional," *Cine Cubano*, Nos. 73/74/75, pp. 80-92.

Viany, Alex, and Joaquim Pedro de Andrade. "Crítica e Autocrítica: 'O Padre e a Moça,' " *Revista Civilização Brasileira*, No. 7 (May, 1966), pp. 251-265.

Viany, Alex, Nelson Pereira dos Santos, and Glauber Rocha. "Cinema Nôvo: Origens, Ambições e Perspectivas," *Revista Civilização Brasileira*, No. 1 (March, 1965), pp. 185-196.